About the Author

Maya Butalid was born in 1957 in Cebu City, Philippines. She studied at the University of the Philippines, where she became an activist against the Marcos dictatorship. She was sent to the Netherlands to work there from 1983 to 1993. She graduated with a Master's in Psychology from Tilburg University, Netherlands. She served as Tilburg City Councillor from 2003 to 2010. She now works with the Netherlands Council for Refugees.

Since 2012 she has worked with *Pasali*, a development NGO in Mindanao, southern Philippines.

She is married to Carlo Butalid; they have two daughters Ligaya and Elena, and grandchildren Tala, Manuel, Noan and Léa.

Chasing Windmills

Maya Butalid

Chasing Windmills

Olympia Publishers
London

www.olympiapublishers.com
OLYMPIA PAPERBACK EDITION

Copyright © Maya Butalid 2022

The right of Maya Butalid to be identified as author of
this work has been asserted in accordance with sections 77 and 78 of
the Copyright, Designs and Patents Act 1988.

All Rights Reserved

No reproduction, copy or transmission of this publication
may be made without written permission.
No paragraph of this publication may be reproduced,
copied or transmitted save with the written permission of the publisher,
or in accordance with the provisions
of the Copyright Act 1956 (as amended).

Any person who commits any unauthorised act in relation to
this publication may be liable to criminal
prosecution and civil claims for damage.

A CIP catalogue record for this title is
available from the British Library.

ISBN: 978-1-80074-086-0

This is a work of creative nonfiction. The events are portrayed to the
best of the author's memory. While all the stories (except for two
essays) in this book are true, some names and identifying details have
been changed to protect the privacy of the people involved.

First Published in 2022

Olympia Publishers
Tallis House
2 Tallis Street
London
EC4Y 0AB

Printed in Great Britain

Dedication

I dedicate this book to my daughters Ligaya and Elena and to my grandchildren Tala, Manuel, Noan and Léa, and to my future grandchildren.

Acknowledgements

I would like to thank my husband, Carlo Butalid, for his unwavering belief in me and for constantly motivating me to write this book. This book would not have been possible without his support.

I would also like to thank the following friends and friends of friends who took the time to read several chapters of my book and provided me with useful and valuable feedback: Amai, Bong, Cora, Dyanne, Ed, Eloise, Ferdie, Girlie, Grace, Honi, Lela, Marco, Maria, Myra, Myrla, Nitnit and Pat.

I also would like to thank Edicio dela Torre for his Foreword; Cor Vulders and Sharon Quinsaat for reading the whole manuscript and providing me with valuable feedback; and last but not least E. F. Uyloan–Germain for her help in proofreading.

Chasing Windmills is a collection of essays about my pursuit of my ideals and principles. My 'windmills' are the challenges that I successfully faced during the various phases of my life. It is a combination of my journey, and my reflections on it.

Contents

Foreword 15
Prologue 17
Chapter 1 Oh Shit 20
Part 1 The Struggle 24
Chapter 2 In the Desert 25
Chapter 3 My Search for God 30
Chapter 4 Life in the Underground Movement 34
List of abbreviations 48
Chapter 5 Acts of Solidarity 49
Chapter 6 The Split 52
Part 2 Being Part of Dutch Society 58
Chapter 7 The Language 59
Chapter 8 A Long Road 65
Chapter 9 The Face of Poverty in the Netherlands 72
Chapter 10 Raadslid in Tilburg 77
List of Dutch words and explanations 90
Chapter 11 Inburgeren in Morocco 92
Chapter 12 **Opstap**: A Child's Learning Begins at Home 99
Chapter 13 A Paradox of Life 106
Chapter 14 The Walk of the World 112
Chapter 15 The Last Ten Kilometres are the Hardest 118
Chapter 16 Musings on my Long-Distance Walks 121
Chapter 17 A Fair Secret 127
Chapter 18 Living with Corona 131

Part 3 Identity 142
Chapter 19 Mama, am I Filipino or Dutch? 144
Chapter 20 Being Allochtoon 155
Chapter 21 On Relationships and Marriage 162
Chapter 22 It is Usual to be a Mother and have a Full-time Job 168
Chapter 23 On Women Emancipation 173
Chapter 24 Musing over a Cup of Caramel Macchiato 177
Chapter 25 Creating and Re-creating Identities 179
Chapter 26 Being a Lola 186
Part 4 Roots 193
Chapter 27 P del Rosario Street 194
Chapter 28 My Mother 199
Chapter 29 Life Happens 207
Chapter 30 Once upon a Time in Heaven 212
Part 5 Touching Base 217
Chapter 31 With Filipinos in the Netherlands 218
Chapter 32 Healing the Wounds of War 224
Chapter 33 *Pasali* and Brain Gain 228
Chapter 34 Together, we can do it 239
Epilogue 241
Chapter 35 Dealing with Life After Breast Cancer 242
Chapter 36 About God 250

Foreword

In *Chasing Windmills,* Maya Butalid shares with us two intertwined sets of stories—the outer stories of the events in her life, and the inner stories of the changes within herself.

At first she set out to write her stories for her two daughters Ligaya and Elena, and their children, her grandchildren. She was getting old and had been diagnosed with cancer.

But she soon realized that she was really writing for herself. She describes her reflections as "a conversation with my soul."

She sent me the manuscript and asked me to write a short introduction. As I read through the chapters, I felt that they are like letters from Lola Maya the grandmother, to her younger self—Maya, the youth activist deployed in 1983 by the Philippine revolutionary movement to do international solidarity work from a base in the Netherlands.

As I read her stories, her picture in my mind is still as I remember her from the 1980s, but her voice in the writings is that of an old soul.

Chasing Windmills has first-hand stories about student activism in the Philippines and solidarity work for the Philippines in Western Europe, the painful split in the movement, and her finding new forms of solidarity work in the Philippines through *PASALI*. These are relatively familiar to me because I shared them in my own way.

What are new to me and fascinating are her stories and insights about being integrated into Dutch society, both as a citizen and as part of local governance in Tilburg. They teach details about the workings of Dutch society and government, not from academic literature but from lived experiences and insightful reflections. They are valuable contributions to those working with migrants, immigrants, and refugees.

Equally valuable are Maya's insights about family, parenting and identity. They are informed by scholarly studies she has done, but they have distinct value as personal stories that capture the emotional tension and challenges. She declares: "I belong to two places: the Philippines and the Netherlands. Both places have shaped my identity. While I am truly 'at home' in the Philippines, I have 'adapted to living' in the Netherlands; but these concepts are difficult to define in practice."

Although she does not refer directly to the central idea of *Sikolohiyang Pilipino* that our identity—*pagkatao*—combines both *loob* and *kapwa*, Maya expresses a kindred idea: "Self-knowledge is achieved not by focusing at yourself but precisely by paying attention to others and to your environment."

Chasing Windmills is a reference to Don Quixote. But instead of riding a horse to tilt with life's challenges, Maya has taken walks, long walks. She has already taken quite a few. And plans to take more. Keep walking, Maya.

Edicio dela Torre

A former Catholic priest who was imprisoned for nine years during martial law, currently works in the field of adult education and participatory local governance in the Philippines.

Prologue

I had the growing urge to put my life story in writing as I grew older. I wanted to write a book for my daughters and grandchildren. I want to share with them the insights I had in life which brought me to where I am now. I want my grandchildren to have an idea where their *Lola* is coming from. But in the process of writing *Chasing Windmills,* I realized that I am actually doing this for myself. In a way, the whole process of writing this book became a process of self-reflection, a spiritual journey.

It was not my original intention to get my book published. But a growing number of friends—during my conversations with them—had been urging me to write a book about my experiences and have it published.

I had been wrestling with the question of why my journey would be interesting to others. Why would someone want to read about my journey?

My journey through life and my reflections on it—from my days as a Philippine political activist, to being a city councillor in the Netherlands, and eventually being involved again in Philippine development, and everything in between—is I think an extraordinary story. I think fellow Filipino migrants would (could) identify with parts of my story. People curious about Filipino migrants' lives could also enjoy the book. For whatever reason people may have to read my book, I hope they will find it insightful, interesting and even entertaining.

Chasing Windmills is a combination of my journey, and my reflections on it. It is as if the insights are the point of the book, and the story is merely a way of conveying them.

Chasing Windmills is a collection of stories of my pursuit of my ideals and principles. The title brings to mind comparisons to Miguel de Cervantes' Don Quixote's (futile) quest for goodness and nobility, where he jousted with windmills, thinking they were giants. My windmills are the challenges that I successfully faced.

I continue to chase windmills. My journey continues... A few words before you read this book.

Chasing Windmills is a collection of articles that I have written on certain episodes in my life. I have done my best to make them:
- short
- easy to read
- insightful
- can stand on their own

The articles are clustered in 5 themes:
- The Struggle
- Being Part of Dutch Society
- Identity
- Roots
- Touching Base

'The Struggle' may be particularly interesting for activists or former activists, or people who are curious about what activists do. Those who have an affinity with Overseas Filipinos (being one or knowing one personally) and immigrants interested in understanding the migrant journey, may find the cluster 'Identity' and 'Being Part of Dutch Society' particularly interesting.

Students of Psychology and Sociology will learn something from those same two sections. Students of ethnic literature (literary works from the perspective of immigrants) may also find the book interesting.

You can read through the book in any order you prefer. You can start with the cluster that you find particularly interesting. Or the articles that catch your eye.

Wherever you start, I recommend that you go through the whole collection. It will be worth your while.

Most articles are based on accounts of aspects or incidents in my life. However, there are two short fiction articles: 'Once upon a Time in Heaven' and 'Fair Secret' which give an interesting twist to the collection.

Enjoy...

Chapter 1
Oh Shit…!

'Knowing you have cancer suddenly makes death have a time frame.'

"Oh shit!" this was my first reaction after hearing from the doctor that I had breast cancer. The possibility of getting cancer had always been hanging above my head as some kind of 'Sword of Damocles'. My mother died of cancer, her two sisters, her brother and her father too. So, hearing that I got it too felt like getting something I had been hoping not to get.

Then followed a short silence, I cried briefly, and I then composed myself as if preparing myself for a major encounter with a new situation.

It was Tuesday afternoon at around three p.m. on June 6, 2017, in the Elisabeth Hospital in Tilburg. My cousin from Rome and my aunt were with us for a visit. That morning I took them for a short sightseeing trip to a castle and a windmill in Heeswijk-Dinther, a town not far from Tilburg. After our short sightseeing trip, we went directly to the hospital for my appointment. I was so confident that the results of the biopsy on my breast would be alright. I even told Carlo to just wait for me, together with my aunt and cousin, in the waiting room of the hospital. But he insisted that he would go with me to the consultation room. Good thing he did!

A week before that, on Monday, May 29, our family doctor called me on my cellphone and asked me if I could pass by her clinic that day. I was then at my work and had several meetings I did not want to cancel. So, I told her that I would come to her clinic first thing the following morning. Our family doctor told me that there were some 'irregularities' seen from the results of my mammogram taken some 10 days earlier. In the Netherlands, women 50 years or older get an invitation from the Population Survey for Early Cancer Detection every two years to have a mammogram for early breast cancer detection. So, this year I had one such mammogram. The doctor told me that the 'irregularities' seen in my breast do not have to mean that I have breast cancer. She wanted to refer me to the hospital for further tests. I wanted to get done with it immediately, so my doctor made an appointment for the following day. The following day, Wednesday, May 31, I went to the hospital for further tests. The hospital had a Mamma Care department where all the expertise on breast cancer were put together. The nurse first did a manual examination of my breast. She did not detect any lump. So, I thought it must be a false alarm. Then I had a mammogram and ultrasound. The radiologist told me that the 'irregularities' were rather small, that probably it was nothing, but to make sure he advised that I have a biopsy done. And it was then that I received the result of this biopsy which I heard from the doctor, a surgeon/oncologist, in the afternoon of June 6, that the 'irregularities' found in my breast was cancer.

Cancer! It sounds so earnest, like the start of a journey towards death. But if I really think about it, life itself is a journey that ends in death. So, what's the fuss?

There was a point in my life many years ago when I declared to myself that I was ready to die any time and face my Creator. I have no unfinished business in this world, and I have lived my life according to my conscience and principles. I believe that the greatest gift God has given us is love and life. And the best way to thank Him for this is to live with love and live life to the fullest possible way, to develop oneself to the best of our ability so that we may be an instrument of God for whatever purpose He had created us. I can say that I have done this. I am at peace with the life I lived, and I am at peace with death.

But why am I then so sad to hear that I have cancer? I realized that it is not the thought of dying which made me sad. As I really looked deep into my feelings, it is especially the knowledge that my death and the process towards it, my fight against cancer, will bring so much sadness to my daughters, my husband, my two sisters and all the other people who are dear to me. Especially the sadness that it would bring to Ligaya and Elena is most painful to me. As a mother, you will always be connected to your children. That umbilical cord connecting a mother to her child in her womb is never really cut. As a mother, my greatest feeling of joy is when my daughters are happy, and my greatest feeling of sadness is when they are sad. My heart is like a sponge that absorbs their emotions.

We all end up in death. We just do not know what the circumstances will be of our death and when it will happen. So, we prepare in general for death. On a spiritual level, I ask myself from time to time the question whether I am prepared to face my Creator. And when I can answer this deep in my heart with an affirmative, then I know I am prepared for death. But of course, I do not want to saddle my family with practical problems arising from my death. So, Carlo knows where I keep our important documents (such as insurance policies and the like), he knows where I have recorded my various codes for different digital portals, etc.

But emotion is something you cannot prepare for. The emotion of sadness my death will cause to Ligaya and Elena, and to Carlo is something I cannot take away from them and spare them from it. And this breaks my heart.

Knowing that I have cancer makes me think differently of death. Death is no longer something which I generally prepare for. Suddenly death gets to have a time frame. Do I live towards it in a year from now? two years? five years? ten or maybe twenty? There was a time in my life when I made a list of what I would like to have done if I only had a day to live, then a year to live, then five years to live, then ten years to live. Suddenly those lists I made are no longer hypothetical, they are no longer wish lists.

In many movies death is often portrayed as a fast-moving series of flashbacks, like a memory lane, of the life of the person who is about to die. Is it time for me to go down my own memory lane?

Part 1
The Struggle

The decision of the University of the Philippines (UP) administration to raise tuition fees by eighty percent in 1977 changed the course of my life. I joined protests against this tuition fee increase; and eventually got involved in the revolutionary movement against the Marcos dictatorship.

What started with my search for God, deepened into a feeling of solidarity especially for disadvantaged people. I was in the movement from when I was a student at the University of the Philippines in 1977, until 1993 after I had given birth to my two daughters and almost finished my Master's in Psychology at Tilburg University.

I did not physically participate in the armed struggle. I did things like organize mass actions in the city and raise political and material support internationally. It was less exciting perhaps, but these were important parts of the overall revolutionary struggle, nevertheless.

I did not join the revolution because it was 'sexy'. It was terrifyingly dangerous, especially since we were fighting a dictatorship; when authorities could pick you up without having to explain it to anyone, and they can do anything to you. I did it because I was driven to do what I felt was the right thing to do.

And I kept at it until such time when the CPP (Communist Party of the Philippines), the leading force of the revolutionary movement, no longer represented the ideals I fought for. It was then that I decided it was the right time for me to leave it.

Chapter 2
In the Desert

'It is noble to fight for one's home, wherever that home may be.'

Late in 1984, I was sitting in a convoy of jeeps and pick-up trucks going through the Sahara Desert. We had travelled for a couple of hours when we came upon an oasis, and we stopped for some needed rest. The desert heat was unbelievable—not only was it very warm, but it was also very dry. Upon disembarking to stretch our legs, people greeted us by pouring a lot of water on our turbans—but within a minute, my turban would be totally dry.

I thought, "This is quite unbelievable. After having stayed for some years in Manila, I had spent a year in (cold) Netherlands, and now I find myself in the middle of the desert. I was travelling, with people I had never heard about even a few months before, as an honoured guest."

A month before, I was sitting in a meeting of the National Democratic Front (NDF) International Office group (which had four members, including myself) in Utrecht, the Netherlands. We were discussing our usual (mundane) stuff; items of news from recent travellers from the Philippines (in that time before the internet, we depended on travellers for news), the coming issue of the 'NDF Update' (our bi-monthly newsletter), solidarity statements that we needed to write and then, invitations and appointments. Usually, we responded to invitations by sending the NDF International Representative Louie Jalandoni or Deputy NDF International Representative Byron Bocar to go. But when we came to an invitation to attend the Congress of the Polisario Front Youth organization (Polisario was fighting for the independence of the Western Sahara), they all looked at me, saying that I should be the one to go.

"ME? I was not an official NDF representative. I had a baby who was barely half a year old. I was too young, etc."

All my objections did not move them. They said that it was a YOUTH Congress, and we needed to send somebody who could represent the NDF Youth Sector and who was young (I was 26 years old, while the other three were already in their 40s). Since I used to be a member of the National Youth Sector Committee of the CPP (Communist Party of the Philippines), and of the youth organization of the NDF (*Kabataang Makabayan*, KM) before I came to the Netherlands, the other three still looked at me as part of the youth sector and should therefore represent it on occasions such as this. Attendance there would be immensely good for our work, since it would widen our international network. My husband, Carlo, can take care of the baby for the 5 or 6 days that I will be away. The experience would do me good. I had no good reason why I should NOT go.

After a short stop, the convoy continued on its way to Tindouf, an oasis which was the main base of the Polisario Front. I was amazed at how they found their way through the desert, with no roads and just endless flat sand.

Tindouf was located on the Algerian side of its border with the Western Sahara. It was practically a city with a school, hospital, and other facilities all mostly in tents. There were also low-lying buildings, like barracks, where we took a nap while the sun was at its highest. Beside each door of the rooms was a big barrel of water. We then poured water over our clothes before taking a nap, only to be dry again before we had even dozed off. One facility that our hosts were exceptionally proud of was a swimming pool!

It was a Youth Congress, so most of the foreign delegates who were travelling with me were young people. The Nicaraguan delegates were the 'cool' ones, because of the Sandinista victory in Nicaragua just a few years before, and everybody (except myself—since I had an aversion for people who behaved 'popular') wanted to be chummy with them. The Palestinian delegates, from one of the more militant factions of the PLO, were always boasting about how they could easily do military acts. The Cuban representative was friendly, but older than most of us. There were only two women in the delegation, the delegate from Yugoslavia and me. Almost nobody had heard of the Philippines or the NDF before.

We were there for a serious matter, to show our solidarity for the struggle of the Sahraoui people for the right to their land and self-determination. But youthful as we were, we were full of energy and were playful. It was natural then for most of us to simply jump into the swimming pool the moment we saw it. It was also natural for me (and some others) to insist on riding a camel when we had the chance to do so. We also took our pictures beside a row of Polisario military vehicles—these were 'technicals' (pick-up trucks with a heavy machine gun bolted to the back)—which we saw parked, ready for the next attack on Morocco.

The sessions of the Congress were held after midnight. People mostly slept and rested during the daylight hours, which were too hot for work.

The Congress had been going on already for a number of days. When the foreign delegations arrived, it was our turn to address the Congress. We each read statements of solidarity with the Polisario Youth. I read a solidarity statement from the *Kabataang Makabayan* (the NDF's youth organization).

The session was followed by a big party in our honor. For the occasion, they roasted a camel, among other things. I could not help thinking that perhaps this was the camel that I rode earlier.

After the party, I went with a group of women to their tent. We chatted, I tried out their clothes, and they decorated my hand with intricate Henna designs. (I thought that the Henna could be washed away immediately; but it stayed on my hand for weeks, months.) I eventually slept with the women at their tent.

The Western Sahara used to be a Spanish colony. In 1975, Spain decided to leave it. Morocco quickly took over, disregarding the wishes of the native Sahraoui population (led by the Polisario Front). In the war that ensued, Polisario set up its main base at Tindouf, on the Algerian side of the border with Western Sahara. From there, they conducted attacks against the Moroccan soldiers, who in turn built a wall (eventually, three walls) to keep Polisario out.

In my short time with them, it was not difficult for me to connect with the Sahraoui people. Except for their clothing they would actually easily pass off as Filipinos, being of medium build and having a slightly dark brown complexion. I found the Sahraoui were a warm people with colourful traditions, and with a deep pride in their identity. I could not help but think "Why would these people choose to live in such a forbidding desert, in order to fight for another piece of the desert?" But then, I realized that they were fighting for their HOME, and that is the most important point. Transferring anywhere else would never be good enough.

The revolution that I was a part of was fighting to improve our HOME, the Philippines. I then realized that I was doing so while living in a prosperous European country. Still, I participated in the Philippine revolution because the Philippines was my HOME; and I wanted to help fix the things that were wrong with it. In a way, I was in a position similar to that of the Sahraouis!

HOME, as I always thought, is where your (core) family is. But as the years went by of living in the Netherlands, with my children and husband with me, I still continued to long for the Philippines, as my HOME. Eventually the Netherlands became my second home. But it is a different kind of home compared to what I feel for the Philippines as my HOME. The Netherlands being my second home means to me that I have found my place in this society and am able to participate fully in it. But when I am in the Philippines, even after so many years of being away from it, I feel like a 'fish swimming in its own waters'. Everything seems so natural, I do not have to think what is proper for me to say and do, which jokes to crack, etc. It all comes out so naturally. This is to me my HOME. And like the Sahraoui people who will continue to struggle until they could be HOME again, I will also continue with my efforts to contribute to the development of the Philippines—a country where there would be peace and justice, and where nobody has to live in poverty—my HOME.

Note: Polisario and the Moroccan government signed a ceasefire agreement in September 1991. They have been waiting since then for a referendum on the status of the Western Sahara.

Chapter 3
My Search for God

'Working for the poor and oppressed is serving God.'

The seeds of my political consciousness were planted by my father. As a young girl I would enjoy listening to his rhetoric until the wee hours of the morning. He would then say famous quotes like "Give me liberty, or give me death!", and "Right makes might". He also admired the bravery of General Patton who fought against the Nazis during World War II.

My father also loved to talk about religion and faith. He was very critical of the Catholic religion: that prayers were memorized so they do not really come from the heart; that some priests who were supposed to live a celibate life, did not; that being a Catholic was not really a personal choice since one is baptized while still a baby. "How could you then know that you want to be Catholic?" He would then say. My father would then give a whole rhetoric about his own search for God. He would then cite quotes from the Bible, such as "Upon this rock I build my Church", and "What you do to the least of my brethren, you do unto me" (note: I am not really knowledgeable about the Bible, so do not ask me where to find these quotes in the Bible).

My father was a very passionate man, he would talk about those things with great passion as if his life depended on them. So as a young girl I somehow also developed that passion inside me the passion to do what is right (as in "right makes might") and go for it (like the fearless General Patton who fought against the Nazis); the passion to fight for freedom when it is taken away from you (as in "give me liberty, or give me death!"); and the passion to seek God, whom I later found among the poor and oppressed in society (as in "What you do to the least of my brethren, you do unto me.").

I brought with me these ideals when I went to UP Diliman (University of the Philippines, Diliman campus) in 1974 as a young girl at the age of 16. In my search for God, I heeded invitations of friends to join their Bible study groups, or to attend their church services. I searched for God in various churches, but somehow, I did not find God in any of them. One thing which bothered me was the claim of each religion that I attended that they are the one and only true religion. Or the preachings that I need to save myself and the only way to do is to accept Jesus Christ in my life, and this acceptance of Jesus Christ in one's life meant joining their religious group. Saving myself as the main purpose for joining a religion sounded very selfish to me. How about helping the weak and the poor? Or doing something good for humanity? Or contributing towards achieving peace, justice and compassion? Are these not a nobler and a more spiritual way to live your life? For after all, God said "What you do to the least of my brethren, you do unto me."

And so, my search for God continued.

In 1977 the school year in UP Diliman started with a surge of students' protests. The immediate reason for this was the high increase of tuition fees which was not previously announced. This caught the students by surprise. Students from far away provinces had to wire (send a telegram to) their parents to ask them to send more money so they could enrol. This provided a fertile ground for the revival of massive student protests. Since the imposition of Martial Law in 1972 there had not been any protests. In my curiosity, I joined these protests.

The protests were about the tuition fee increase. But soon enough the student leaders talked about the curtailment of the people's democratic rights and about the amassing of wealth by the then President Marcos. Soon enough the student leaders talked about the military atrocities across the countryside, and the victimization of the poor people in particular. My eyes were opened, never to be closed again, and my view of Philippine society was broadened. I realized that the social problems I saw in the neighbourhood where I grew up as a child were actually just a representation of what was really happening in the rest of the country. I continued to attend those political symposiums and rallies, especially to learn more.

In August 1977, an international conference of lawyers was held in Manila. The student leaders saw this as an opportunity to bring to international attention the human rights violations being perpetrated in the Philippines. A big student rally was then organized in the heart of Manila, in Arroceros. This was attended by thousands of students from various universities in greater Manila. I also joined this protest rally. (By the way, my parents attended this international conference of lawyers, both of them being lawyers.) This protest rally turned out to be my first direct experience of police brutality. The student demonstrators were dispersed by the police using water cannons. However, due to the presence of international media, nobody was arrested. I went back to my dormitory in UP Diliman all wet and soaked but fired up with what just happened.

Not long after that, my dormitory roommate told me that there was an underground movement of youths and students fighting for the overthrow of the Marcos dictatorship, and to restore democracy and justice in the Philippines. In those days, when you are against the government you are immediately labelled as subversive. So, all organizations against the government had to operate 'underground' (meaning secretly). My roommate invited me to join this underground youth movement, the *Kabataang Makabayan* (KM). And I thought to myself, "This was something I could be passionate about—to fight for freedom, to fight for what is right, and most especially, to fight for the plight of the poor and oppressed of Philippine society". These were the very seeds that were planted by my father in me as a young girl and which guided me in my search for God. Suddenly, all these fell into place. There was this movement of people who fought unselfishly for all these, unmindful of the possible dangers of being incarcerated or even summarily executed for doing so. People with tremendous commitment for a noble cause. I wanted to be part of this movement.

And I thought to myself, "I guess I have found God."

Chapter 4
Life in the Underground Movement

Life, love and laughter in a revolutionary movement.

It was past midnight, at the crossing of EDSA and Muñoz Market. We were pushing our car, which did not start after having stopped before a red traffic light, trying to get the engine to run again. We were all sweating, not because of the warm weather, but because we were in front of a police station, and our car was full of revolutionary documents and anti-government propaganda. We had to clear our UG (underground) house from these materials as there were indications that our house might have been under surveillance. And of all places, the car's engine broke down in front of a police station! Who would not get nervous at that? Luckily, it did not take too long for our car to start again. So, we proceeded to the place where we could keep our materials for safekeeping. Later, while unloading our boxes full of materials, one of the boxes gave way and the materials were strewn on the road! While this was indeed an alarming situation at the time; we would go into uncontrollable laughter whenever we would talk about it later. Indeed, looking back, what happened then was almost like a scene in a slapstick movie, where everything that could go wrong did go wrong.

It was in August 1977 when I joined the underground movement (*Kilusang Lihim*) against the Marcos dictatorship. *Kilusang Lihim* or *KL,* which literally means 'secret movement', was the collective name of all CPP (Communist Party of the Philippines)-led organizations, such as the youth organization *Kabataang Makabayan* or *KM*, the particular organization I joined. This was after I joined several student rallies and demonstrations mostly inside the UP Diliman campus as part of the surging student protests against the sudden increase of tuition fees that school year. Later, these student protests tackled not only the tuition fee hike but were also directed against President Marcos and martial law. After attending a big student rally in the heart of Manila, in Arroceros, which was dispersed forcefully by the police using water cannons, my roommate told me that there was a secret movement fighting against the Marcos dictatorship and invited me to become a member. And I accepted. This was the start of my activism and life in the underground movement.

As an activist, aside from joining and mobilizing others to join rallies and demonstrations, we would also hold so-called 'lightning rallies'. This is comparable to what we now call 'flash mobs'. During these 'lightning rallies' a group of activists would suddenly assemble in a shopping area or busy street and chant slogans against the Marcos dictatorship, then disperse before the police arrive. This action takes about 5 minutes.

Sometimes, we would also hold 'mass distribution' actions. A whole group of activists, each with a pack of printed anti-government materials, would simultaneously step into classrooms and give the pack of materials to the student seated nearest to the door (with the instruction on paper to "get one, and pass the rest"). We would also have *Operasyon Dikit* or *Operasyon Pinta*, in which we would either stick revolutionary posters on walls, or paint slogans. We did this at night when there were less people on the streets. I personally pasted posters; but during *Operasyon Pinta* I only served as a look-out.

I would often work as a 'runner'—bringing messages or leaflets in and out of school buildings and demonstrations. I guess I was asked to do this because of my innocent-looking face; one which the security guards would not suspect to be an activist. During demonstrations, I would carry messages between the demonstration's 'Central Command' and the 'Higher Organ' outside. In those times there were still no cell phones, so messages were literally transmitted verbally through 'runners' like me. Working as a 'runner' for big demonstrations in which I needed to deliver messages from the 'Central Command' inside the demonstration to the 'Higher Organ' outside it, and vice versa, was one of my favourite tasks in the underground movement. The 'Higher Organ' would usually meet in a relatively fancy restaurant, to avoid suspicion from police agents. And of course, I also had a chance to eat with them, which I considered a treat.

Gradually, my activism began to take their toll on my studies. In June 1980, I decided to quit school and go full time for the revolutionary movement. A few months earlier (in March), Carlo and I got married. Soon after going full time, we moved into a UG house rented by our collective (at that time, our collective was the one in charge of the underground network in the University of the Philippines—Diliman, College of Arts and Sciences). When I later became the head (Secretary of the Party unit) of the underground movement for the whole of UP Diliman, we moved to the UG house of that collective.

UG House
A UG (underground) House made our work more efficient, since our collective could just meet there, instead of having to find a place to meet every time. We needed to be careful about our

security though. In the first place, we had to have a credible story for our landlord and neighbours. Then, we needed to keep the UG House secret, not only from the military and police, but also from our Lower Units. Perhaps because of their youth, they made it a sport to try to find out where the UG House of their Higher Unit (i.e., our house) was. We would often take circuitous routes before going home (e.g., suddenly leaving a jeepney, and then riding another one in the opposite direction) to avoid being followed.

We had a security policy to stay in a particular UG House for a maximum of six months. We therefore had to constantly change UG houses. We kept our furniture and personal belongings to a minimum so that moving from one UG house to another would be easy. Well, in a way, this was also in line with our principle of 'simple living and hard struggle' (*simpleng pamumuhay at masigasig na pakikibaka*). My personal belongings back then would fit in just a small hand-carry bag, just the basic necessities. I also did not keep pictures of myself, family and friends, one of our precautionary security measures, just in case our UG house would be raided by the police.

One of our security policies was also that if a member of our collective, or our political officer or 'PO' from our Higher Organ, would get caught; we had to leave our house immediately. For such cases, we agreed on certain signs to warn our collective members not to proceed to the house anymore (e.g., a towel would be hung from the window). Subsequently, we would ask personal friends (i.e., non-activists) to empty the house for us.

UG names

As members of the underground movement, we took on 'UG names', as we had to conceal our true identity for security reasons. I had several UG names—Joesen (this was actually my father's nickname), Carmen and Georgia. I liked Georgia most of all, it has something boyish in it. So, I used this name for quite a long time and many comrades still remember me by this name. When I went full time for the movement, I only went home to my parent's house in Cebu during the Christmas holidays. One time my mother called me (of course with my real name) and I did not respond. She came to me and asked me why I did not respond to her calls. I then realized that I was no longer used to hearing my real name. I found that rather funny.

When Carlo and I went to the Netherlands I automatically took on a new UG name, Maya. But the reality in Europe is different, there is no need to conceal my identity, there is freedom of speech and gathering support for the struggle of the Filipino people against the Marcos dictatorship was allowed by law. So, in the course of time, Maya became my real nickname. So, what's in a name?

From candidate member to full member
After a year of being a member of the CPP-led organization *Kabataang Makabayan or KM*, I was invited to be a candidate member *(kandidatong kasapi or KK)* of the Communist Party of the Philippines (CPP). This was in August 1978. A year after that, in 1979, my Political Officer (PO) told me that my 'trial period' of one year was over and that I could already become a full member (*ganap na kasapi, or GK*). But then I had to pledge adherence to the principles of the CPP, one of which is the principle of dialectic materialism. An important aspect of this principle is being scientific. In particular, this would mean that my belief in God would run counter to this principle as there is no scientific proof of God's existence. While I was not really very

religious (I hardly attended Holy Mass), but I could not take it upon myself to say that I no longer believed in God. Deep in my heart I still did believe in God. In fact, it was my search for God which brought me to the movement. So, I told my PO then, "It is okay, I do not have to be a full member." Still a year later, in 1980, my PO told me that I really needed to be a full member as I was already assuming responsibilities which required being a full member. This was the time when I became the head of the whole underground network in UP Diliman. My PO told me then "It does not matter if you still believe in God. It is okay." And so, I became a full member in August 1980. I was the first in our collective (who were all KKs) to become a full member, so my comrades in our collective would fondly call me "jik", referring to *GK (Ganap na Kasapi)*.

Meetings
When we had meetings with other units, we could not have them in our UG House (and neither in the other unit's UG House), so we met elsewhere. For shorter consultations, we would meet at an eatery. The disadvantage of this was that we had to order something, and our financial resources were very limited. We would also often meet at a park: preferably one where one would need to pay only a small fee to get in e.g., the Chinese Garden at the Luneta, or at Fort Santiago. When meeting at a park, we would often recognize other UG groups also meeting there. For longer meetings, we would meet in the house of a friend.

Sometimes we would need to go into a school to have a meeting, or to coordinate a demonstration. There were security checks at the entrance of the schools, but we found ways to enter anyway. We would sometimes find a way to get a student ID; or show a receipt of registration and say that the ID was not yet finished; or sometimes I would rush in pretending that I was already very late for my exams. I guess because I was petite and had an innocent-looking face I easily got away with those tricks.

Wedding

My most memorable event was our 'revolutionary' wedding. We had previously already been wed twice: before a judge on March 7, 1980, and then in church on June 10, 1980, but we also wanted to have a revolutionary wedding. It took some time for our request to be married inside the revolutionary movement to be processed. We were then the first couple from the Youth and Students sector to wed, so our higher organ had to pass our request to their higher organ as they did not have any experience yet with such requests. So finally, in November 1981 our marriage inside the movement was officiated. Arrangements were made for about 20 guests (from various units) to attend. We had to be careful regarding security measures (since such a big gathering would be a big 'catch' for the security forces). As we were the first couple from the Youth and Students sector to have a movement wedding, it was a very special event, especially for the guests from our lower units.

The wedding was done in a church, where the priest was a *kasama* (a fellow activist*)*. It was the perfect cover. We agreed that if government agents came in, the priest would simply tell them that we were getting married. The priest was among the guests, but the wedding was officiated by somebody from the Higher Organ (actually, he was someone from 2 levels up since nobody in the whole Youth sector was yet authorized to officiate). The wedding started with us relating the history of our relationship, with questions and comments from the guests. There was an explanation (homily?) on the role of married couples in the revolutionary movement. And finally, there were the wedding vows. When the ceremony was over, we had a 'reception'—eating all the food brought by the guests.

Relationships

Young activists, by their nature, would naturally get attracted to members of the opposite sex (at that time, same-sex relationships were frowned upon). But courtship in the underground had some distinct characteristics. The initiating party (which could be male or female) would ask her/his PO to contact the PO of the 'target' activist for permission to start a courtship 'program'. If the person agrees, then courtship would start. When actually courting, the initiator needs to first declare her/his basis (*batayan*) for proposing the relationship. Activists generally ask for the basis before entertaining any proposal. The basis is supposed to be mainly political, and only secondarily personal. Personal basis referred to personal characteristics such as one is beautiful/handsome or 'cute', and these were generally considered shallow and not enough to start a relationship.

If there is more than one person interested to court the same comrade, only one courtship program was allowed at a time; suitors should await their turn. There was a time when three members of our unit, including me, each got a request from a member of our respective lower units, all women, to court a male comrade from another unit, the PO of whom was also in our collective. So, the three of us had to formulate the basis for courtship together with the requesting female comrade. It was then up to our unit to decide who would be the first to court based on the basis that was formulated. The female comrade in the unit under me honestly told me that she really just found this male comrade very attractive and handsome, and that she was afraid that she could not really come up with a strong political basis why she should have a relationship with him. I told her, "Do not worry, I'll help you formulate your political basis." I guess we did well together in formulating her political basis as she got the permission to be the first one to court. We really had a great laugh while deliberating on the various political basis submitted by the requesting female comrades. It was quite obvious that those political bases were actually more our work—their respective POs—than of the suitors themselves. So, in a way it was 'my victory' over the other two POs in my collective.

There was a strict prohibition of sex (i.e., sexual intercourse) before marriage. When some would do it anyway (and got caught) there would be a 'trial' which would end up with punishment which was usually a 'warning' (*babala*) or a 'severe warning' (*mahigpit na babala*). Nobody ever got punished with demotion or expulsion for this kind of offense. Some *kasamas* who had been punished would say "I do not mind the warning, it was worth it."

But others took to heart the puritanical prohibitions. Once, a woman from a lower unit confessed that she had kissed a *kasama* who was not her boyfriend and expected to be punished. Our unit simply brushed this off. But there were other units where this would have been taken seriously.

Finance, Parents
How did we support ourselves financially at this time? Carlo and some of his friends had set up a typing business at the UP Shopping Centre. Typists would type up papers for students, for a fee. The typists would keep half of the income; while the other half went to supplies, typewriter maintenance, rental and the profit for the investors. Carlo managed the business; and one of

the partners contributed all of his profit share to us. Our income from this was substantial; it took care of most of our personal needs.

The rental cost of our UG House was covered mostly by the dues and contributions of lower units. Then, all of us had a network of friends who would support us with food and money, and sometimes a place to sleep.

Carlo's and my parents lived in Cebu, while we were in Manila. We did not receive any financial support from them after we went full time. They mostly disapproved of our activism. Once, when I was still studying, my father threatened to prohibit me from returning to Manila. But when he and my mother realized that I had arranged to go back to Manila with or without their permission; they accepted that I was going back.

I told my parents that it was I who had recruited Carlo into the movement. Carlo told his parents that he had recruited me. So, neither of our parents could blame anyone but their own daughter/son for our activism. (Actually, we were recruited separately, at almost the same time.)

I would go to Cebu during the Christmas break. Before I went full time, I also went home during the semestral break. My short stays in Cebu were generally pleasant. I did not argue with my parents about their views. I accompanied my mother when she went to buy groceries and to church. I was back to being the obedient child I had been except that I would not agree to stop with my activism. Choose your battles, so to speak. Before I would return to Manila, my parents would give me new clothes.

Serious Business

When I joined the movement, I did not give a thought about how dangerous this might be. All I thought about was the need to fight against the Marcos dictatorship and for national freedom and democracy. Until the time when we got news that the boyfriend (who was also an activist) of a woman comrade in our collective disappeared and was later found dead with signs of having been tortured. This news really struck me. I felt sympathy for the loss of my woman comrade, but I also realized for the first time that this could also happen to me. I gave it a serious thought and decided to continue with my involvement in the movement.

Like me, anyone who joined the UG was aware of the seriousness of what we were doing—that we could be arrested (or worse) at any moment. We went about our daily work conscious that there were government agents constantly on the lookout for us. Whenever we left our UG house, we were never sure if we would see the members of our collective when we came home, or if we would come home ourselves. This was especially worrying for me—not knowing every time, if this would be the last time, I would see Carlo. When we would quarrel (and I think this was often) in the evening, we had to reconcile before sleeping (which meant sleeping very late) because we did not want to separate angry with each other the next morning.

While Carlo and I were never caught by the police, we had our share of alarming moments. One of them was when we were still renting a room in the UP Diliman campus. Our landlord informed us one day that they got a visit from somebody from the UP police force while we were away, who asked them to open our room so they could inspect it for subversive materials. Luckily, our landlord and landlady were sympathizers and they refused to do so. We had to immediately give up our room and sleep several nights with friends until we found another place to rent.

Another incident was when some student activists of a

university where Carlo was the PO were arrested. Upon release they told Carlo that their interrogators had shown them his picture. They had seen him around, but that he was not registered as a student in that school, and that they suspected that he was the person from UP (the police assumed that the movement's leaders all came from UP) assigned to lead the UG in the school. And they were right! He had to take extra precautions when going near that school from then on.

Consenting PO
At a certain point I became a member of the Regional Commission of the Youth and Student Sector in Metro Manila. After having been the head (Secretary of the Party unit) of the UG network in UP Diliman, I acted as a political officer (PO) to the UG units in some schools outside of UP Diliman. I was then the PO of the High Schools unit and the collectives of various exclusive schools. A collective of one of the exclusive schools for girls was quite critical of anything coming from the Higher Organ. Their previous PO was very strict with them and was very critical of their 'bourgeois' way of life. So, when I met them for the first time—it was an overnight meeting in one of their houses—they wanted to provoke me. Before we started with our meeting, they told me that they first wanted to watch a Betamax film. In those times 'Betamax films' meant porno videos. To their surprise I just said "Okay" and watched the Betamax film with them. That was how I established rapport with them as their PO.

During that time, many student and youth activists somehow hold a 'romantic' view about the armed struggle being waged by the New People's Army (NPA, the armed wing of the CPP) in the countryside. Many student and youth activists dream to someday join the NPA. A member of our high school collective submitted such a request to me as his PO and asked me if I could give a positive recommendation to his request. I declined, telling him that I did not think that he was ready for that. He asked me why. I told him that he did not even have the discipline to do his tasks here in the city, how much more when he is in the countryside in more difficult life conditions? "I think you are romanticizing the armed struggle, and that you have really no idea how it is to live a simple and hard life in the countryside", was what I told him. He got really pissed off with me and told me that I was not acting like a PO. "Any PO would welcome such a request", was what he told me.

During our evaluation of our strengths and weaknesses we would make a headcount of all the activists under our jurisdiction. We would then categorize the activists into three categories 'advanced, middle and backward' elements. We would also note the number of 'lie-lows' (i.e., those who left the movement). Of course, one of the tasks at hand was how to make the 'middle and backward elements' into 'advanced', and how to prevent the 'backward elements' from lying low. Some POs would then try to talk especially to the 'backward elements' to motivate them to be more active in the movement. As a PO, this was actually not my cup of tea. I believe that we all joined the movement with our eyes open, knowing what we were getting into and whatever else motivated us to get involved. So, I also believe that we all also have our own reasons for leaving it. We are all grown-ups, and we can think and decide for ourselves. So, when comrades tell me that they wanted to leave the movement I was always okay with it. I accepted and respected their decision, I never made any effort to convince them to stay.

Somebody once commented to me that I was a consenting PO. I guess I was.

Summing it up, life in the underground movement was not all hard work. There was also lots of laughter and fun. And love was able to find its way in between the hard work and dangers we faced. While we adhered to certain principles (which may lead to dogmas), in the final analysis it is the individual person who decided for himself/herself how to live by those principles.

List of abbreviations

CPP – Communist Party of the Philippines
EDSA – Epifanio de los Santos Avenue, road running from north to south of Metro Manila
GK – *Ganap na Kasapi*, refers to Full member of the CPP
KK – *Kandidatong Kasapi*, refers to Candidate member of the CPP
KL – *Kilusang Lihim*, secret movement, the collective name of all CPP-led organizations
KM – *Kabatang Makabayan*, Nationalist youth, the youth organization of the CPP
PO – Political Officer
UG – Underground
UP – University of the Philippines

Chapter 5
Acts of Solidarity

'Being inclusive is being in solidarity.'

It was the day after we had a children's birthday party in our home for Elena, my youngest daughter. I do not exactly remember which year it was, but Elena was about seven or eight years old and still in the first few years of her elementary school. A friend of hers, who was also at the party the previous day, came to our door. She wanted to return some stuff she borrowed from my daughter. Elena was not at home, so I just took the plastic bag with the stuff in it: some coloured paper, a pair of scissors, coloured pens, glitter things, ribbons, paste, etc.

Later that day, when Elena came home, I told her about the stuff. I asked her "What are these for?"

To which she answered nonchalantly "Oh, it's my stuff which I lent to her."

"What for?" I continued.

"Oh, I wanted to invite her to my birthday party, and she first did not want to come saying that she did not have any money to buy me a birthday gift. She was ashamed to come to my party without having any gift. So, I lent her some stuff and told her to just make a beautiful birthday card for me."

"Hhmmm" was all I could say.

"You see" Elena continued, "she does not really get invited to birthday parties by the other girls of my class, and I thought if

I will invite her to my party, then my other friends will also do the same." I thought to myself "Wow! This is solidarity in its purest form."

The first time I encountered the concept of 'solidarity' was when I came to the Netherlands in 1983 to help in the international work of the National Democratic Front (NDF) of the Philippines. An important part of our international work was to gather solidarity support for our struggle against the then Marcos dictatorship in the Philippines. At that time solidarity work for various so-called third world countries was quite popular among the Europeans. There was also then a European network of solidarity groups for the Philippines, which was quite extensive, covering most Western European countries.

The NDF was often invited to speak during the meetings of these various solidarity groups for the Philippines. As part of the NDF group for international relations I had my share of speaking during some of these meetings. I would then talk about the political situation in the Philippines and the state of affairs of the NDF's struggle for a democratic and just Philippine society. I did not only speak to solidarity groups for the Philippines, but also to other political organizations of Europeans, such as political parties (mostly left), organizations of women, workers, etc.

The concept of solidarity was to me then political, specifically gathering political support for the struggle in the Philippines. Reflecting on it, it was mostly quite one-sided, towards the direction of support for the Philippines. Of course, we also regularly issued solidarity statements for the struggles in other countries. But it felt then as some kind of a protocol, express solidarity for others as part of our political work but also to gain solidarity from them.

But what does solidarity really mean? To me, solidarity is

supporting each other, being able to recognize each other's connectedness, being inclusive, and acting upon it.

At her young age Elena somehow already understood what it really took to be in solidarity. She acted on the basis that nobody in her class should be excluded.

Another instance of an act of solidarity was when my eldest daughter, Ligaya, was in high school. There was a group of 'popular' girls in her class who constantly made fun of and bullied a boy in her class. She thought that this was not right. So, she convinced her friends to go with her to the rector of her school and tell him about this. The rector spoke to the class and the bullying stopped. I found out about this through the rector during one of those parent-teacher consultations. When we asked Ligaya about it, she simply shrugged and said "Oh that. Yes, I thought it was not right to make fun of and bully others, so I had to report it."

"Weren't you afraid that those other girls, who are popular in your school, will bully you in turn?"

To which she said, "No, I am not afraid of them."

I never thought that I would understand the essence of solidarity from this unexpected corner, the simple acts of solidarity, on a person-to-person level.

Chapter 6
The Split

'Politics is personal.'

It was April 24, 1993. More than a hundred people gathered in a restaurant at the centre of Utrecht, the Netherlands, to listen to Byron Bocar, the National Democratic Front (NDF) representative for Western Europe. Meetings like this had been held for years on this very date, to mark the anniversary of the founding of the NDF in 1973. But this year was different. It was the day when the NDF organization in Western Europe, together with NDF committees in the US, in Asia, and the Philippines declared that they had split from what they called the 'Stalinist' NDF led by Jose Maria Sison. These NDF committees declared themselves as representatives of the true NDF—the part of the NDF that upheld democracy and was seriously committed to implementing the NDF's program. The Philippine press even dubbed this grouping as the *Verdaderos*—those standing for truth.

As a member of the NDF Executive Committee for Western Europe, I had a humble part in preparing for this day.

A few years earlier, the NDF organization in Western Europe started a program of democratization among its ranks. It moved away from methods that had been transplanted from the Philippines—with its secretive and highly centralized way of working. We applied democracy and transparency throughout the structures that the movement had set up in Western Europe: the solidarity network, the NDF organization, and even the CPP (Communist Party of the Philippines) organization were all transformed. Members were enthusiastic about the changes. By the end of 1991, the process was essentially completed: all our leading committees had been elected, and policies were decided upon democratically.

In December 1991, Jose Maria 'Joma' Sison wrote the paper 'Reaffirm Our Basic Principles and Rebuild the Party'. It was a call to roll back all the reforms that we had implemented thus far. In response, we called for two big meetings in Utrecht in January and February 1992 to discuss it and other related papers. Out of more than forty members in those meetings, only four fully agreed with Joma and the paper. After February, Joma no longer participated in any meeting to discuss the paper. The debate continued in the form of position papers and memos, until early in 1993.

Our official break with Joma Sison and his dominant faction of the CPP-NDF was not only a big political event; it had personal consequences for Carlo and me. The split meant that the monthly allowance that we received from the movement was suddenly cut off. This was a very trying time for both of us since we had to find money to support ourselves and our two daughters. For the next six months we had to borrow money to make ends meet. I realized then how many real friends we had; we were able to borrow money from people we did not expect. We were pleasantly surprised.

While we were struggling to make both ends meet, we were able to acquire permanent residency permits in August 1993. This made it possible for me to apply for a regular job. In September, the program where I had been doing my practicum had an opening for a regular job, as a coordinator of the program. I applied for the job and was accepted. I was able to work starting in October and received my first salary at the end of that month. This, and the financial help we got from friends in those very trying months, made me realize that God, despite that I had not given any attention to my faith and spiritual life for years, had always been there with us, looking after us.

While the official split happened on April 24, 1993, my feeling that the CPP was no longer my party had actually already started much earlier. I do not consider myself an ideologue; so, I did not really participate actively in the debates by coming out with position papers and the like. To me politics is personal. I believe that one's politics should be consistent with how one lives her/his life. That one should walk the talk. Sadly, enough, I did not see this in the leadership of the CPP.

The day after Nelson Mandela, the South African liberation leader, was released from prison after twenty-seven years of imprisonment on February 11, 1990, I came across Joma Sison on the bus on my way to our office in Utrecht. "Did you see it on TV last night? Mandela's release from prison and how happy the South Africans were? I'm really so happy and excited for the South African people", was what I told him, still excited about the news from South Africa.

To which he promptly said that "our movement missed the opportunity to organize massive celebrations, similar to South Africa, when I was released from prison." Suddenly all my excitement was gone, and I realized that our movement had a leader with delusions of grandeur.

One time we had a meeting in Joma's house. I was then part of a small secretariat staff for Joma, which happened to be all women. Julie, Joma's wife, was also there. I can still remember how Joma 'commanded' Julie to take such and such a document from his files *("Kunin mo nga iyong ... papeles.")* or to bring him coffee *("Kape nga Julie.")*. I was so tempted to say to him "Could you please say please?" As we were all women in our staff we also talked, during our break, about what we can do to pursue women empowerment and emancipation. And Julie blurted out that there is no need to take action towards this, because once socialism will be achieved the women will be automatically empowered and emancipated. This was actually quite a let-down for me. While I may not consider myself an ideologue, I had already come to the conclusion that the emancipation of women would not automatically happen when socialism is achieved. Socialism is about the economic structure. While the economic position of women is important to achieve emancipation, I believe that the emancipation of women also had a cultural dimension—that is, getting rid of the patriarchal system and the deep ingrained sexism present in our society. So, if the leadership of the Party does not see the point of taking women emancipation on board in its struggle, how could it be my Party?

I could go on with a lot of examples of incidents leading to the erosion of my belief in the leadership of the CPP. But I will not do that. It will not serve a purpose, and it does not really matter to me now.

In the 1980s there were also other solidarity networks for several countries with a liberation struggle, like Chile, El Salvador, East Timor, etc. We then also got to know them. In particular, we built a friendship with a member of the Communist Party of Chile who was then living as a refugee in the Netherlands. We met every week; he would give us Spanish lessons and we shared experiences about our respective liberation movements. One thing which really struck me was how the

Chilean liberation movement really put democracy and transparency in practice within their ranks. The CPP-led liberation movement in the Philippines was very top-down. We would just get policies for implementation from the higher organ, with a minimum of explanation. And when we asked for more explanation, we would just get a general answer that it was not possible to share all information due to security precautions. As an activist I just accepted this. After all, we operated 'underground' for security reasons. But when I heard about the efforts the Chilean liberation movement made to discuss matters as widely as possible within their organization, I realized that the Philippine liberation movement was actually just lazy, taking the easy way of just using 'security reasons' as an excuse not to discuss policies extensively within its ranks. So how could we then implement democracy and transparency in the government we want to set up in the Philippines if we ourselves do not practice them?

Being in Europe also exposed me to what was happening in the rest of the world. In the 1990s for example, war was going on in the former Yugoslavia. The news about it was almost every day on television. There was so much destruction, misery and suffering. And I thought to myself, "is armed struggle really the solution to the problems in the Philippines?" The CPP is also waging an armed struggle through its New People's Army (NPA). I realized that it was such a big responsibility to call for an armed struggle, considering the destruction it may cause to human lives and property. "And when we topple the government, what guarantees do we have that what we put in its place will be a better one?" I remember what Joma told us in one of those meetings we had in the heat of our debates, that we have been contaminated with the western way of thinking and have thus stopped being revolutionaries and turned into reformists instead. Or was it 'revisionists'? Yes perhaps, but those labels did not move me anymore. I guess it was around this period when I stopped living according to dogmas, and simply acted based on my inner compass.

It was August 1977 when I joined the CPP-led underground liberation movement in the Philippines, and I left it in April 1993. This is sixteen years of my life! Do I have regrets? Did I waste those sixteen years of my life? Not at all! I learned a lot in those years. I learned to be critical, but in a constructive way. I learned to analyse the various problems of society and think of solutions. I developed a deep affinity for the poor and disadvantaged sectors of society, for humanity, for what is right and just. It was in those years when my inner compass was developed. I also developed deep and lasting friendships with a lot of comrades, comrades who fought passionately for their ideals.

And when I no longer believed in the CPP, when I realized that the CPP was no longer my party, I left it without any hesitation, even if it meant losing our financial support. So no, those sixteen years of my life were not wasted years. Not at all!

Part 2
Being Part of Dutch Society

Anybody who lives in the Netherlands is, strictly speaking, part of Dutch society. You buy groceries and other things in local shops; your children go to Dutch schools; you encounter people in all kinds of social occasions, etc. But truly becoming part of Dutch society involves conscious acts, e.g., learning the language, attending parent-teacher meetings, joining a club or political party. Foreigners learn Dutch words e.g., *goedemorgen* (good morning) or *dankjewel* (thank you) quite readily; but really learning the language usually requires some formal education.

I was required, to be able to stay in the Netherlands, to master the language to university level within one year. This was because I supposedly planned to study in a Dutch university. So, I did. But for the first ten years of my stay, I was mostly involved in the Philippine movement—my friends were mostly those Dutch who were active on the Philippines; I did not take part in most events of the bigger Dutch society.

Getting my permanent residency permit in 1993, my split from the Philippine revolutionary movement and acquiring Dutch citizenship in 1994, changed things for me. I got a job, and with this exposure to more ordinary Dutch and mainstream Dutch society. I got more involved with my children's school. Eventually, I got involved in Dutch politics, and became city councillor in Tilburg.

All these made me realize that I have become an integral part of Dutch society.

Chapter 7
The Language

'Language is a means to connect, communicate and participate in the society you are in.'

It was October 1983. Carlo and I were at the train station in 's-Hertogenbosch, waiting for our connecting train to Tilburg, where we lived. There were a lot of people also waiting for the train to Tilburg, when we heard over the public address *"de trein naar Tilburg, Breda en Roosendaal van zestien uur vierendertig heeft een vertraging van tien minuten, en zal aankomen en vertrekken van Spoor 4"*.

We had arrived in the Netherlands in August and did not yet know much of the Dutch language. The transport workers were launching wildcat (i.e., unplanned by the unions) strikes, which were causing disruptions in train services.

Upon hearing the announcement, most of the people who had been waiting for the train with us started moving away. Panic! What is happening? We hurriedly asked one woman who was moving away. She answered, "the train will leave from Platform 4". Thankfully, we were able to catch our train. But the feeling of panic and helplessness lingered for a while. It was such an awful feeling, I never wanted to feel that way again. Never again! It made me realize how important it was to learn the Dutch language.

Learning and mastering the Dutch language has become an

important on-going thread, even to this day, in my life as a migrant here in the Netherlands.

When we came to the Netherlands in August 1983, we only had tourist visas. For us to be able to stay longer, we had to change our visas. It was possible for us to acquire student visas IF we enrolled in the university the following schoolyear (i.e., by September 1984). We therefore only had a year to learn enough Dutch to qualify for admission to the university. We did not follow a language course, but just used the audio lab lessons at the university and did a lot of self-study. We subscribed to a newspaper (de Volkskrant, one that used high-level Dutch), watched TV programs which had Dutch subtitles, watched the daily news on TV for children (as the language was formal but simple), and talked to our friends and neighbours as much as possible in Dutch. All these efforts bore fruit as we both passed the Dutch language examinations in all four categories of reading, listening comprehension, writing and speaking in August 1984—just in time to enrol in September.

When we started the process of changing our visas early that year, the Alien Police informed us that I did not need to enrol at once at the university. That if Carlo got a student visa, I could stay on the basis of being his partner. The Alien Police saw that I was pregnant. Even with this knowledge I still continued to learn the Dutch language to qualify for admission to the university. Just in case Carlo would not be able to make it. I gave birth to my first daughter, Ligaya, in March 1984 and decided to forego my enrolment to the university.

Even if I did not have to study in the university, I continued to feel the need to learn the Dutch language. As a mother I wanted to be able to understand and communicate with people and institutions relevant to my children, such as the community nurses and the nurses of the well-baby centres where I took my children for regular check-ups, the caretakers of the day-care centres where my children went to, their teachers when they started going to school, etc. In a way, after passing my Dutch language examinations in August 1984, my progress in learning the Dutch language went side-by-side with the growth of my two daughters, Ligaya and Elena. As a mother I did not settle for just understanding the language. I asked questions and spoke out during parents' meetings in their day-care centre and schools. I also sought interaction with the parents of Ligaya and Elena's classmates, so that our children could play with each other after school. In the Netherlands children do not just go to each other's houses to play. They first have to make appointments with each other, or rather their parents do.

In September 1988, it was my turn to enrol at the university and acquire a student visa. At the start I tended to take notes in English during lectures. But soon enough I realized that it was easier to take notes directly in Dutch, as the lectures were in Dutch, rather than keep translating what I heard to English. During my first exams as a student many of my professors were so kind and told me that I may answer the questions in English. But the part of me who loves a challenge decided to do my exams in Dutch. Besides, I did not want to get special treatment. As the saying goes "When in Rome, do as the Romans do." My mastery of the Dutch language made some progress during my student years.

In October 1993 I got my first job in the Netherlands as a project coordinator of a parenting program in an institution for social work in Tilburg, where I lived. Soon enough I was confronted with the feeling that my mastery of the Dutch language was not enough. During meetings I found it so frustrating that I would still be formulating in my mind how to say my points in Dutch, and the meeting had already moved on to the next topic. I then decided that I should improve my mastery of the Dutch language to a higher level. I looked for an advanced Dutch language course and found one. With the information I gathered about the course, I went to the head of my department and to the head of our Personnel and Human Resource Department. My employer agreed to pay the tuition fees and books for the advanced Dutch language course I wanted to take, and the transportation expenses, as the course was in another city. I wanted to do the course in my own time, not as work time. I told my employer that the course was not only directly work-related but was also part of my personal development. I therefore also wanted to invest personally on it as a matter of principle. My mastery of the Dutch language again made progress as a result of this course.

Formally studying the language is essential should you want to master it. But a lot of learning and mastering happens in the actual practice when you use the language in your daily life—as a mother, at work and by simply participating in the society where you are in.

It also requires an open attitude to learn a language—knowing when you need to improve your mastery of the language and allowing others to help you. When I just started working in 1993, I asked the secretariat department of our office to check all my outgoing letters for any grammatical errors. I always then compared the original version of what I wrote with the final version made by the secretary, to see the mistakes I made. I also allowed my children, and still allow them, to correct my Dutch when I talk to them. And up to this day I still consult every now and then the dictionary; and I even have a dictionary of idiomatic expressions.

Learning a language also requires courage, the courage to use it actively in your daily life and not allow yourself to be limited by your imperfect mastery of the language. When Ligaya was in the elementary school, either in Group 4 or 5 (equivalent to Grades 2 or 3), I volunteered in their class for their reading activity. I saw in their school newsletter that they were looking for parent-volunteers for various school activities, and one of them was for their reading activity. I then asked her teacher what the parent-volunteer had to do for this activity. And she told me that they have this so-called reading hour when the children can choose a book to read silently. And if there were words they could not understand, they could go to the parent-volunteers present in the class who would explain to them the meaning of the word. "Hhmmm, do you think I can do that?" I asked the teacher.

"Well, I can understand you very well, and I think you have a wide enough Dutch vocabulary. So, yes, I think you can do it. Just try," was what she said. And so, I did! My insecurities about the language were unfounded.

There were always more children who lined up in front of me, than in front of the other parent-volunteer. I guess they were just amused with me because of my different accent. I would see them smile while I was talking with them.

Learning to master a language also requires endurance. During my first few years as a student in the university I would go through my Dutch textbooks at least twice. During the first reading I would take note of all words I did not understand. I would then look them up one by one in the dictionary and made notes of the meaning of the words. Then I would read again the text to be studied with my notes of the words I looked up in the dictionary at hand.

Having achieved a high level of mastery of the language, I have written reports and other official documents in Dutch. Because of the grasp I have of the language, I am able to participate in discussions at work and meetings or debates during my time as a city councillor from 2003 to 2010. I also prefer to read novels and instruction manuals in Dutch than in English. So, I am really quite comfortable with the Dutch language, having been able to internalize it to a certain level.

But I know that my Dutch is not perfect. It is also not my intention to have a perfect mastery of the Dutch language. Mastering the language is not an aim by itself, but language is a means, an instrument to connect, to communicate and to participate in the society where you are in. So even if I make grammatical mistakes or speak with an accent or mispronounce some words; these do not stop me from speaking my mind. I would always tell myself, "I have made a lot of effort to learn the Dutch language, so it is not too much to expect from the Dutch people I talk to also try to meet me halfway by trying to understand what I am trying to say despite the imperfections of my Dutch language."

Being able to understand, speak and write the language in the society you are in as a migrant is actually very liberating. It helped me to be an effective mother, it allowed me to make my own choices and fully participate in this society.

Chapter 8
A Long Road

'I realized that a Master's Degree would help me find my place in the Netherlands.'

It was August 1999 when I had finally submitted my Master's thesis 'The acculturation of overseas Filipinos in Belgium, Germany and the Netherlands'. It had taken me eleven years to get to this point from when I started studying Psychology in August 1988, with two majors, Children and Youth and Cross-Cultural Psychology, at the Tilburg University. I did not actually spend eleven years at it: lectures and class work ended in 1991, and I did my practicum in the school year of 1991–1992 and started with the research for my thesis in the succeeding school year 1992–1993. But then I got immersed in my new job and other activities, and the thesis got 'frozen' from late 1993 to mid-1998. Every year I would register as a student, in the hope of finishing the thesis that year, but nothing happened.

Until August 1998, when I decided not to enrol anymore—I had lost hope of ever finishing the thesis and graduating. Out of the blue, I bumped into one of my professors (my practicum adviser) while buying groceries. He encouraged me to finish my Master's thesis; and to put action to his words he immediately made an appointment for me with the student adviser of the Psychology Department in our university. So, I had to go to that appointment. The student adviser immediately put me in contact with my thesis adviser. I was so ashamed to go to his office, having not done anything about my thesis for so long. But my professor was so happy to see me. He told me that I was really so close to finishing my thesis, so it would really be a pity to give it up. Actually, he was right about that. I had already collected all my data, had ran several statistical analyses on it and had already written several pages of my thesis. So, I decided to enrol one more time in September 1998, and made a commitment to myself this time to really go through with it and finish my thesis. When my former classmate and friend (who was then already working on her Psychology PhD, under my thesis adviser) heard that I was going to resume working on my thesis, she immediately called and offered to help me through it. And to put action to her words she immediately made an appointment with me on a regular basis to discuss my thesis and its progress. Because of this I regularly came to the university in-between my working days, and this really helped a lot to keep the momentum going. It felt good to be back. I realized that I actually missed the academic life. When I think about the circumstances around the finishing of my thesis and finally getting my Master's diploma in Psychology, it was actually that chance encounter I had with my professor which triggered everything and put things into motion. It may be simply a case of serendipity, but to me it felt like the 'forces of the universe' had worked together to help me get my diploma.

In 1992, when I proposed to do research on acculturation (i.e., adjusting to another culture) of overseas Filipinos I wanted to cover six European countries which included Italy, Spain and England; countries where there is a concentration of Filipino migrant workers, and Belgium, Netherlands and Germany; countries with a concentration of Filipinas married to host country nationals. I wanted to compare the acculturation strategies of these two groups of overseas Filipinos. I thought that if one is a migrant worker then probably one has no intention to live in the host country permanently, and if one is married to a host country national one's framework is to live in that country permanently. I was interested to see if there was any difference in their acculturation strategies. But my thesis adviser said that such a topic was too big for a Master's thesis. "You are not doing PhD research, just a masters", was what he told me. So, I trimmed down the scope of my research to three countries instead, Belgium, Netherlands and Germany. For the requirements of my Master's thesis it was sufficient to cover only overseas Filipinos in just one country, the Netherlands, for example. But I was brimming with enthusiasm, and since I had actually worked with overseas Filipinos in all three countries, I managed to convince my professor that covering the three countries was manageable.

I also wanted to gather data from undocumented overseas Filipinos. But in the course of gathering data from them (through my network) I got into contact with several undocumented overseas Filipinos) one of them asked me what my purpose was to also include the group of undocumented overseas Filipinos in my research. "Will the results of your research on us come out with concrete proposals how our situation could be improved?" was what he asked me.

"Well, not really. I just want to know how the group of undocumented overseas Filipinos respond to another culture, if it would be different from the overseas Filipinos with stay permits," was what I answered. "The results of my research on this may lead to some insights which could be useful."

And he said, "You know what, I will answer your questionnaire because I want to help you with your studies. But I also want to let you know that being 'invisible' is actually our only protection. So, the least attention we get in the open, the better for us." And this really struck me. I believe that as a social researcher my research should contribute to address a 'social problem'. But if this is not the case, then I do not have any business 'poking' into the lives of a group of people simply just for knowledge. Knowledge should serve a purpose, and in this case a social purpose. So, while I had several respondents to my questionnaire who were undocumented overseas Filipinos, I did not take them as a separate group in my statistical analysis. I think their 'invisibility' should be respected.

I designed a questionnaire for the overseas Filipinos and asked my contacts in Belgium and Germany to distribute them to their network. These contacts were operating within institutions that helped Filipinos in these countries. I had an extensive mailing list of Filipinos in the Netherlands which I used. The questionnaire was made in conversational Tagalog or 'Taglish' (i.e., with some English words mixed in). The questionnaires were sent with a pre-paid (i.e., with stamps), pre-addressed envelope. I sent out a total of 684 questionnaires, and I received one hundred and thirty-eight completed questionnaires back (approximately twenty percent response).

And then, other things in my life caught up with me. 'The Split' in the movement happened, and our source of finances suddenly vanished. Luckily, Carlo and I got our permanent residency permits in August 1993, having already stayed for ten years in the Netherlands. With a permanent residency permit one is already allowed to work. Shortly after getting our permanent residency permits, there was a job opening at the institution where I had done my practicum. Again, a case of serendipity. I applied and was accepted; I started working in October. The work was challenging, and it consumed all of my time and energy. But since I was so close to finishing the thesis and graduating, I registered as a student in September 1993, and again in 1994, 1995, 1996, 1997—always in the vain hope of finishing my thesis that year.

My findings

The research had a limited sample size (one hundred and thirty-eight respondents) out of a total overseas Filipino population of more than a hundred thousand in the three countries. So, any findings would have to be called preliminary, or as a basis for further research. The findings, however, provide meaningful insights that are relevant for work among overseas Filipinos.

First of all, it found that language skills are important for integration. While this sounds obvious, now I had data to back such a view. Institutions serving overseas Filipinos (especially those who had recently arrived) could help them a lot by providing language training facilities or by encouraging them to learn the language as soon as possible.

Second, membership in Filipino organizations seem to play a valuable role in the integration process of overseas Filipinos. This seems counter-intuitive; many people (especially host country nationals) think that migrants should associate less with their own countrymen and instead mix more with nationals of the host country. But another way of looking at it is that membership in Filipino organizations provide a secure base from which overseas Filipinos could establish relationships with the host culture, and this in my opinion facilitates integration.

Third, the central issue in the acculturation process of overseas Filipinos is whether they should retain or shed their original culture. The issue of establishing and maintaining relationships with the host culture seems to be a secondary concern. In my research, integration appeared to be the most preferred acculturation strategy of overseas Filipinos in the three countries studied. By integration one opts to maintain one's cultural identity while moving to become an integral part of the larger, more dominant host society.

Surprisingly, my research showed no significant difference between assimilation and marginalization. I know that I sound like I am giving a lecture here in cross-cultural psychology, but please bear with me for a while as this is really important. Often migrants are told by host country nationals 'to integrate'. But what is actually often meant with this is for them to assimilate, meaning that they should behave as host country nationals do, letting go of their original cultural identity and opting to move to the larger, dominant host society. But what if one has already 'shed off' her/his original cultural identity but failed to replace it with that of the host society's culture? Then marginalization occurs, wherein the person experiences a feeling of alienation from both societies. The results of my research seem to back this up, having no difference shown between assimilation and marginalization. A food for thought for overseas Filipinos who think that the best way to participate in the host society is to shed off ones 'Filipino-ness'. Be careful, as you might just lose yourself instead.

The whole long and agonising road to finishing my thesis and graduating was influenced by the fact that I had, in a sense, been studying my own situation. The years 1993 to 1999 were the years when my own process of acculturation went into high gear. It was only after I left my activist life in 1993 that I was fully confronted with having to find my place in Dutch society. My getting a regular job intensified that process; and it was partly the reason why I did not pick up my studies/research for such a long time. My eventual realization that a Master's degree would help me fully find my place in the Netherlands, probably provided the final push for me to finish my studies.

My thesis adviser called in his last comments so I could rework my thesis and still be able to submit it on the last working day of August 1999. If I, did it any later, I would have had to enrol again for another school year.

Chapter 9
The Face of Poverty in the Netherlands

'Many Dutch do not realize that there are also poor Dutch.'

"Summer vacation is 'sacred' in the Netherlands, but people living in poverty do not take vacations." I made this statement during the Tilburg city council meeting of May 22, 2006, when the council was deliberating the setting up of a city Task Force on Poverty. The Task Force was scheduled to come up with its findings by the end of September 2006, which was necessary in order to include them in our budget deliberations for 2007, which would take place in November 2006. But July and August were summer vacation months. So, some city councillors of other political parties proposed that the deadline be moved to a later date since the end of September was not realistic, because most city councillors would be on vacation.

As a Task Force on Poverty, we wanted to talk to as many people in Tilburg who were facing poverty, to get a deeper understanding of it and thus be able to come up with concrete recommendations for eradicating poverty in the city. If we wanted to talk to many people, we had to continue working through the summer vacation months. In my mind I could not take it upon myself to tell the people living in poverty who cannot afford vacations that they will just have to wait a while before we could talk to them, because we would be on vacation. Nobody could present a counter-argument, and so it was decided that the

Task Force on Poverty would commence with its work immediately and would go on working through the summer months.

As a city councillor for the Dutch Labour Party (*Partij van de Arbeid, PvdA*) I was the party's spokesperson for social concerns such as poverty. I was therefore part of the Task Force on Poverty which was then being set up. This experience broadened and deepened my understanding of poverty. My understanding of poverty in the Philippines was quite straightforward, that is that people who are poor do not have the financial means: to have a decent home (or are even homeless), to eat three meals a day, to get an education to qualify for a relatively well-paying job, to go to the hospital or to take medication when they get sick, etc. Poor people were those who did not have the means to provide themselves with the basic things in life. When I came to the Netherlands, I saw that all these basic things in life—house, education, health care, basic income for food—were all taken care of by the government, the Netherlands being a welfare state. So, I thought that there was no poverty in the Netherlands.

When I started working in a Dutch institution for social work in 1993, I worked with so-called socially disadvantaged communities in Tilburg—communities with lots of migrant families, lots of unemployment and lots of people living on government welfare. I saw for the first time how it was to be poor in the Netherlands. It is indeed not like in the Philippines, since they have the basic things in life, but in a way, it was not really better. I remember telling myself then that I would rather live as poor in the Philippines than as poor in the Netherlands as long as I am healthy (because the Netherlands has a good universal health care system).

Who are these poor people that the Tilburg Task Force on Poverty wanted to talk to? These are people, who have been dependent on welfare money from the government for so many years; those who were not able to avail of income-support services from the government simply because they did not know about them or because their particular situations fell outside the scope of these services; those who have huge unmanageable debts; the so-called working poor (those with jobs but do not earn enough); the youth who no longer went to school but were unemployed; single parents with young children; old people who have small pensions, etc. While these people may have a house to live in, a basic health insurance, and were able to send their children to school (as education is free but compulsory up to 16 years old); what they have in common is that they have to struggle each day to make both ends meet. They do not have any money for the extras. And what are these extras? To hold a birthday party for their children, to go on vacations or even just a day out to relax, to have a hobby, to join clubs, etc. When you think about all these, they seem to be the luxuries or extras. But are they really extras? What happens when you are not able to do them? If a child could not hold a birthday party, she does not get invited to birthday parties of children in her class. She could then be socially left out in her school.

In one of the house visits by the Task Force on Poverty, we talked to an old woman who lived on a small pension. She had always been a housewife. When her husband died, all she got was a small amount for widows. She told us that she was really very lonely, and that she spent much of her time alone in her house. We asked her if she tried joining a club with other people of her age. She said that this was too expensive for her. It was not only the membership fee which she could not afford, but also spending on coffee or tea every time the club meets. She was also wary that she may get invited by others to their houses for coffee or tea. "Why is that?", we asked her.

"Because I will then have to invite them back for coffee and tea too, and I do not have the means for that.", was her answer. Yes, these are seemingly simple things, but they have quite a big impact on the person.

We are all social beings, we need contact with people. Social contact is a basic necessity of life. But if you are poor in the Netherlands, chances are that you live an isolated life and thus are deprived of that one big basic thing, that of being with other people.

Another dimension of living in poverty in the Netherlands is the fact that it is mostly hidden. There is generally a taboo about living in poverty. People try to hide it. Poor people are ashamed that they will be judged by others that they are poor because of their own doing. I can imagine that the shame of being poor is real. I remember the first time I saw a homeless person in the street, I thought to myself "If you are poor in this country then it must be of your own doing. Everything in this country is provided for by the government. You really need to fumble big time with your life for you to become poor." Yes, I too was judgmental towards poor people in this country.

During our work in the Task Force on Poverty we talked to a homeless person. He told us that it was his choice to be homeless, that it was his way of life. "Why is that?" we asked him.

"I do not want to be part of the system. I reject the system and all its rules," he said. We did not argue with him. We told him that we respected his opinion. But we asked him if he would give it a try and allow the government to help him. And if he did not like it, he can always go back to his life as a homeless person. He agreed! I saw him a year later. He was no longer homeless, he looked well groomed. He spoke in one of our social commission meetings of the city council, during the evaluation of the policies we made on addressing poverty. "I am actually quite content with my life now. Through my work I get to meet new people and even get to help other people too. This gives me a feeling that I am doing something useful with my life," was what he said.

So, this person only thought it was his choice to be homeless; but given a chance, he actually preferred a regular life.

Yes indeed, this is also one aspect of being poor in this country, eventually losing your self-worth. By being poor you are in a constant struggle to make both ends meet, you then become consumed in your personal situation. This, combined with a lack of social contact, could result in your alienation from society. And if this goes on for too long, you will eventually lose your self-worth. I believe that as social beings we need other people to give meaning, and thus worth, to our life.

So having said this, I think that the material poverty that I knew in the Philippines is not really worse than social poverty that I have seen in the Netherlands. Poverty has many faces, and I would not wish anybody to live in any form of poverty. For me, helping eradicate poverty in all its forms, wherever in the world, is a noble thing to do and to strive for.

Chapter 10
Raadslid in Tilburg

My experience of being a city councillor

Candidate, Campaigning, Elections
Sometime in 2001 I had a meeting with the party leader of the Dutch Labour Party (*Partij van de Arbeid*, *PvdA*) in Tilburg, Jan Hamming, who was also an alderman in Tilburg. I thought that he wanted to talk about the parenting program I was coordinating in several neighbourhoods in Tilburg. Earlier that year I had talked to him about it, to get his support. But when I talked to him, he told me that the reason why he wanted to speak to me was to encourage me to run for the coming local elections for city councillors in 2002, under the party list of the *PvdA*. (In the Netherlands, the mayors are appointed.) He saw that I was very involved in the communities where I was working and told me that the party needed socially engaged people like me. So, I applied to be in the *PvdA* party list, and ended up quite high on the list for a newcomer to the party.

I participated in the campaign for the 2002 elections. Campaigning was labour-intensive, going house-to-house in various neighbourhoods distributing our pamphlets at areas with a high footfall: the train station, shopping centres, even schools (when parents drop off and collect their children) and old people's homes. We also gave out red roses, which symbolized the *PvdA*. There were no big *miting-de-avances*.

On election day, people would go to a precinct, present their ID or passport, and vote. In municipal elections, foreigners who had been residing in the country legally for at least five years are also allowed to vote. The voters would then choose one among the various parties (the party lists were arranged in the order of the seats the parties held in the previous council; *PvdA* was then list number two, being the second largest *fractie* then). After having chosen the party, voters then chose a candidate within that party's list.

After the precincts closed, the votes were counted there, and transmitted (at that time, a diskette was brought by hand by the precinct head) to the city hall, where they were tabulated. The precincts closed at eight p.m. and by about ten p.m. the results were out. The parties were allotted seats based on the proportion of the vote that they got, and these seats are alloted to the candidates. For example, if there are 40 seats, and our party got 25% of the vote, it will get 10 seats, which will go to candidates No.1 to No.10.

I did not immediately enter the council after the elections, but I was the one next-in-line to be in the council if any of the *PvdA fractie* members stepped down for any reason. In April 2003, a *PvdA raadslid* (councillor) did step down, and I succeeded him as *raadslid*. I was sworn into office as city councillor in June 2003.

One of the things I did when I found out that I was to be a *raadslid* was to inform my sister and father in Cebu about it. They were very happy for me. My father had run for Cebu City councillor many times (always as an independent, and never won), so I told him that I had finally succeeded where he had not. He replied that things are different in the Netherlands, where elections are honest.

Being *raadslid* in the Netherlands is different from being a city councillor in the Philippines. I was just one of thirty-nine council members (the size of the council depends on the population of the city, at the time of this writing Tilburg already had forty-five council members). It was a kind of parliament for the city. The day-to-day running of the city was done by a then seven-member body called the *College van Burgemeester en Wethouders (College van B&W)* composed of the mayor plus six aldermen coming from the ruling coalition. The *College van B&W* serves as the Executive Council of the City Council.

In the Netherlands no single party runs the government, it is always a coalition of several political parties, which together form a majority of the council. The political party who won the greatest number of seats would then take the lead in forming the coalition government. It then invites other political parties, on the basis of political party programs, to sit with them to discuss if it is possible to form a coalition government among them. Negotiations ensue, each political party 'putting water to the wine' to each of their respective programs. The resulting government program is then a result of these negotiations.

We worked mainly by *fractie*—the grouping of council members from the same political party. I was a member of the *PvdA fractie*. We divided the work within the *fractie* and determined together our position on policy questions.

I was assigned to join two council commissions: *Maatschappij* (Society) and *Economie* (Economy). Within these commissions, the specific topics for which I was assigned as first spokesperson (*eerste woordvoerder*) for the *PvdA fractie* were for the following areas: social work, social welfare, youth, emancipation, global awareness, labour market and employment. This meant that whenever an agenda point fell in the topic where

I was the first spokesperson, I would have to prepare for the discussion of this topic in the *fractie*, and if needed, I would be the one to present the *fractie*'s standpoint on that topic during the meetings of the commission and/or the council's plenary meeting.

There were two other commissions: *Fysiek* (Infrastructure) and *Moderne Bestuur* (Modern Management, which dealt with complaints or appeals from the public).

Topics

The council discussed a wide range of topics: from big topics like our annual budget or development plans for the city, to really small ones e.g., someone wanting to open a repair shop in a residential zone. Topics first get discussed in the various commissions before they are presented to the council. Then, the commissions' recommendations are given to the council members (for them to read). Simple questions, such as the repair shop question above, were then put among the first points in the agenda of the plenary session. The chairperson of the plenary (the mayor) would then read the agenda points one by one, and if nobody objected (for the simple questions), the recommendation of the commission would be approved, and the chair then pounds the gavel, closing that topic. This is why such simple questions are called *hammerstukken* (gavel pieces).

The *Openbaar Vervoer Plan* (Public Transportation Plan), which specified the bus routes and schedules for Tilburg was discussed at length by the various communities in Tilburg. After all, if a bus route is changed, or a bus stop moved, people are quite affected. When this topic was discussed at plenary, it was quite lively. There were a lot of people wanting to address the council with their concerns and suggestions for the plan, and the public gallery was quite full. After the plan was approved, the city held an auction among bus transport companies to determine which would run the buses in Tilburg for the next five years.

Budget Deliberations

The biggest topic that the council discusses every year in November is the city's annual budget. The budget at that time was over seven hundred million euros per year. And that for a city of just over two hundred thousand people. More than half of the budget goes to social support e.g., unemployment support, help for people with a handicap, helping people to become self-reliant, etc. Other big items were for urban development, management of public space and the police. More than half of the budget comes from the national government; the rest is generated from local taxes and other sources e.g., income from sports facilities, parking fees, etc.

The budget deliberation is actually my favourite council meeting. The *College van B&W* submits its budget proposal to the council. During this meeting we go through all policy fields for the coming year, looking into the proposed budget allocations for each policy field, but also for each and every budget item under each policy field. Two things could happen, either we approve the proposed budget allocation or come up with concrete counter proposals. It is a very direct expression of our priorities for the coming period.

Counter proposals are either to scrap a specific budget item, or allot a bigger budget allocation on a specific budget item, or include a new budget item not allocated in the budget proposal of the *College van B&W*. When a *fractie* brings up the need to allot something, they also have to present which item(s) in the proposed budget need to be scrapped in order to make space for it. We are not allowed to make uncovered budget proposals, as the whole budget has to balance. We call this 'budget discipline'. These proposals may be agreed on immediately, but in most cases extensive debates ensue as each political party wants their party program to get implemented.

In preparation for the deliberations, we needed to thoroughly read the whole budget proposal (which goes into hundreds of pages). First, we needed to see which of 'our' items were not funded, or insufficiently funded. Then, we also need to find items we wanted reduced or scrapped.

The deliberations usually went on until the wee hours of the night. We would go home often at around two or three a.m.

Spokesperson

In the two commissions which I participated in; I presented our *fractie*'s position on the topics that I was assigned as first spokesperson. In the Social Commission, one point that I presented, for example, was the need to set up higher-level language lessons in the neighbourhoods. The existing system was to have low-level language lessons in the neighbourhoods and higher-level language lessons done centrally. Many *allochtoon* (i.e., migrant) women with small children, who wanted to take higher level language lessons, could not go all the way to the other side of Tilburg for these, as they had to be on time to fetch their children from school. As a result of my input, a senior civil servant approached me after the meeting to discuss possibilities for doing this.

As spokesperson on matters related to the integration of newcomers (i.e., refugees and other migrants) to society, I also participated in a project for 'reverse *inburgeren*' (civil integration), in which Dutch policymakers went to Morocco to experience being integrated there (See Chapter 11). I gained a lot of insights into how a person feels while going through the civil integration process; insights which I was able to subsequently bring to the council to improve the civil integration program in Tilburg.

I also suggested that Tilburg do something to help women, who are not considered breadwinners, to find a job. The government had been helping men who were unemployed to get jobs, in line with the 'breadwinner policy' of the government, through various programs, but not their wives. But many of their wives also wanted to work. I argued that work would help these women (many of whom were migrants) to integrate, and also become more emancipated.

When I became a councillor, the *Wet Werk en Bijstand* (*WWB*, Employment and Support Law) had just been passed by the national government. The *WWB* basically transferred the responsibility for promoting employment and supporting the unemployed from national to local governments. This was in order to allow greater flexibility. In practice, it was an immense addition to the work of the council.

The *WWB* was part of one of the topics I was assigned as first spokesperson, and was one of the first that I had to handle when I came in. Since I had come in 'late' to the council, discussions on this topic had already started in the commission before I came in. In order to catch up, I attended a lot of seminars held at national level on the topic. When I attended the commission meeting, I was pleasantly surprised to discover that I knew more about the topic than the representatives from some other political parties. As a result, I contributed a lot to the discussion on implementing the *WWB* in Tilburg. (The mayor specifically cited me for my many contributions to the *WWB* discussions during the ceremony when I left the council in 2010.)

Combatting poverty in Tilburg was a big part of my area of concern. I started with pointing out that the *AOW* (basic subsidy for old people) was too low. According to a study, they have a structural deficit of seventy euros per month. Later, I pointed out that there were many people whose salary was equivalent to the level of the *Bijstand* (minimum social security subsidy). Also, that poor people were not able to join clubs or associations and tended towards social isolation. Tilburg had a system of giving a one-hundred-euro subsidy to poor people so that they can participate in some social activities. (Our family had availed of this subsidy sometime in the 1980s. We used it, among others, to pay for swimming lessons for Ligaya.) But there were many who did not avail of this, and other subsidies aimed to help poor people.

In 2006, the council decided to form an Anti-Poverty Task Force. The Task Force needed to talk to as many poor people as possible and had to do this before the budget deliberations later in the year. This meant that we had to do a lot of interviews during the summer vacation months of July and August, and some political parties suggested moving the deadline because they did not want to do this. I told them that poor people did not have vacations and are we to tell them to wait because the council members would go on vacation. Nobody could present a counter-argument, so it was agreed that the Task Force commence work immediately and go on working through the summer months.

I participated in a number of interviews (see Chapter 9) and the discussions to process these. We were able to submit our report in September 2006. And this could be included in the budget deliberations in November of that year.

Integrity

In the council, we were very conscious to avoid conflict of interest or corruption in various forms.

Since I was then working for an NGO for Refugees, which was partially funded by the city government, I recused myself from that part of the session whenever there was an item concerning our NGO and refugees. Other councillors did the same when it applied to them. This is to avoid a conflict of interest, or even just the impression that there was a possible conflict of interest.

We are also required to report when we receive gifts as councillors worth more than twenty-five Euros. We end up refusing to accept most such gifts.

Once, when a casino operator (from another city) wanted to open a casino in Tilburg, he invited the whole council to go to his casino. But the council refused (after some discussion) because this could be construed as a bribe by the casino-owner to sway the decision of the council. The council eventually refused to give permission to open the casino in Tilburg.

I wonder when our politicians and policymakers in the Philippines will reach this level of integrity in the performance of their public functions.

Working Visits

As councillors, we also went on working visits within Tilburg, and sometimes even to another city. When I was only a few weeks in the council, we had a working visit to Maastricht. We went to see how their city council worked; and it was also as a kind of 'team building' for us.

In Tilburg, we also visited homeless shelters, working spaces provided for amateur artists, new housing projects, elementary schools (while the budget for education comes from the national government, the construction and maintenance of elementary school buildings are the responsibility of the local government), etc.

One peculiar experience I had was on a visit to a *gebruikersruimte* (users' space) in Tilburg. This is a place where addicts can turn in their empty used syringes for a new one and inject heroin in peace. This kind of place would not be allowed in the Philippines, much less get a subsidy from the city government to operate. The idea behind this 'users' space' is to prevent addicts from stealing to get money for their addiction. Also, by providing a place where addicts can exchange their used syringes for new ones helps prevent the spread of HIV/AIDS and other diseases. Many cities in the Netherlands, especially the big cities, have *gebruikersruimtes*. The Dutch are known for their tolerance and for being practical. The Dutch policy regarding the setting up of *gebruikersruimtes* for its addicts is a fitting example of this characteristic.

Load

The work in the city council was quite heavy. In addition to the monthly council plenary session, I also attended the monthly meetings of two commissions and the weekly meetings of the *fractie*. In addition, the *PvdA* had also set up workgroups of *PvdA* party members to stimulate their participation in the work of the council. I was a member of three of these workgroups, for Labour, Welfare and Multicultural. These add up to ten regular meetings a month. There were also invitations to events by organizations supported by municipal funds.

Preparation for the meetings took a lot of time. Every Wednesday and Friday we received the materials that we needed to read. These materials, which ran into hundreds of pages, needed to be read before our *fractie* meeting on Tuesdays. This meant that we spent a lot of time during the weekend just reading all the materials.

All in all, I had meetings and working visits three to four times a week, plus lots of time for reading and other preparations. And I did this in combination with my regular job.

In 2006, I ran for a second term as *raadslid*. This time I was able to enter the council immediately after the elections. I served until March 2010.

Learning Experience

Being a councillor and spokesperson on certain topics made me learn how to formulate and express standpoints (in Dutch) very quickly. I prepared my initial comment on the topics in advance (this took a lot of time initially), but then there were rebuttal rounds in which I had to formulate on-the-spot our *fractie* position and reaction to the positions of the other political parties. In the beginning, other members of the *fractie* helped me to do this, by passing me notes on what to say. But later, this was no longer necessary as I was able to formulate the rebuttals by myself.

My experience as councillor has shown me that citizens have many opportunities to influence policies. There are many consultations at the neighbourhood and city level, which are held by the various commissions, in order to find out the opinions of the people. If you want, you can request to speak during commission hearings. The schedules and topics of consultations and hearings are published in our local newspapers and are available in the official website of the council.

During the discussions on the bus routes and schedules for

example, I noticed that the sixty plussers (sixty years or older) were very much present. They were present in all the consultations on the topic. They were able to get changes in the original plan as a result of all this. On the other hand, youth and *allochtoon* (migrant) citizens were hardly present in these consultations.

I learned that the different parties in the council had real differences in their standpoint on various topics. Most of our discussions and debates really revolved around political party programs. For instance, in a discussion on a housing project, the *PvdA* was pushing for a bigger percentage of social housing, while the *VVD* (Right Liberals) wanted more houses designed and built for the middle and upper section of Tilburg's populace. And while *PvdA* kept pushing for higher parking fees (to stimulate people to use public transportation), the *VVD* and *CDA* (Christian Democrats) insisted on 'affordable parking'. *Groen Links* (Green Left) would comment that everyone should just come by bike, which is best for the environment. In the end the parking fees remained unchanged, as a compromise.

The discussion about parking fees came back almost yearly during the budget deliberations. I never thought that such a topic would be a hot issue among the political parties.

Another rather big discussion we had in the council was about the proposed plan to build a big shopping mall just at the edge of Tilburg. *Groen Links* was against this plan as it will bring more traffic towards Tilburg, and thus worsen the air quality of Tilburg. The *VVD*, which has many supporters from the local business sector, was worried that the shopping mall would take business away from the local businesses. Within the *PvdA fractie* we also had a lively discussion on the topic. While we understood the position of *Groen Links* regarding the effect the shopping mall will have on the air quality of Tilburg, we also realized that the shopping mall would provide job opportunities for Tilburg's populace. Finally, we in the *PvdA*, true to our being a Dutch Labour Party, voted positively on the proposed plan to build a big shopping mall in Tilburg. In the end, it was not passed. Personally, I was not really keen to have a shopping mall in Tilburg. You might think that as a Filipina I would like to have a shopping mall in Tilburg, being used to the many big shopping malls in the Philippines. But what I specifically like in the Netherlands are its *gezellige* shopping streets, with each city and municipality having its own characteristic shopping street.

For the local elections in 2010, I decided not to run for another (third) term. I thought, it is time for me to move on and make room for others. I was part of the *PvdA* selection committee which screened the line-up of candidates for our party list for the elections of 2010.

My last council meeting was on March 10, 2010, which was a farewell meeting for all non-returning council members. In his farewell speech addressed to me, the then Mayor Ivo Opstelten of Tilburg said the following (in Dutch):

"We have known you as a socially engaged person. A councillor that stood up for the weak of society, with your participation, among others in the council's working group Taskforce Against Poverty I and II. You were very involved in the formulation of our policy framework on the *Wet Werk en Bijstand* (*WWB*, Employment and Support Law). You were not only a good people's representative but were able to translate what you saw and heard from the people into policy proposals. The past years were not always easy for you, this due to the health problems of your husband (note: Carlo was bedridden from early 2008 to late 2009). But despite this, you continued with your involvement and efforts for our city."

Glossary

allochtoon – migrant
AOW (Algemeen Ouderdom Wet) – Law on Basic Pension
bijstand – social support given to people without income
College van B&W (College van Burgemeester en Wethouders) – Executive Committee of the City Council composed of the Mayor and the Aldermen from the ruling coalition political parties
Commissie Economie – Commission for Economy
Commissie Fysiek – Commission for Infrastructure
Commissie Maatschappij – Commission for Societal matters
Commissie Modern Bestuur – Commission for Modern Management
eerste woordvoerder – first spokesperson
Fractie – group of council members under the same political party
gebruikersruimte – users' space, referring to a room where drug addicts can use their drugs
gezellig – nice and cosy sphere
Groen Links – Green Left, one of the political parties in the Netherlands
hammerstukken – gavel pieces, agenda points which are readily voted upon without further deliberations
inburgeren – civil integration

Openbaar Vervoer Plan – Public Transportation Plan
PvdA (Partij van de Arbeid) – Dutch Labour Party
raadslid – city councillor
WWB (Wet Werk en Bijstand) – Law on Employment and Social Support

Chapter 11
Inburgeren in Morocco

'In order to really understand them, you should walk in their shoes.'

Newcomers to the Netherlands undergo a program of *inburgeren* (civil integration). Some years ago, the Dutch government formalized the program of *inburgeren*, with government-funded courses (on language and about Dutch society) and an exam.

The project *'Inburgeren in Marokko'* on May 7 to 13, 2007, was '*inburgeren* in reverse', where people involved in social work and local government in the Netherlands went to Morocco to experience what it was like to *inburgeren* there. This was in order to get insights that would help improve the program of civil integration in the Netherlands.

I joined the project because I wanted to understand how one could undergo civil integration when one is 'other literate'. Arabic (which is the language in Morocco) was for me not only another language; it was an 'unwritten' language (in the sense that their letters were totally alien to me). Later, I realized that civil integration is much more than just learning the language.

I participated in the project as a city councillor and aimed to gain insights that would help improve local civil integration policies. Furthermore, being foreign-born myself, and previously having been a newcomer to the Netherlands, I could also share with present-day newcomers the attitude and effort that are needed to succeed. The bottom line is that newcomers themselves are responsible for the success or failure of their own civil integration. I would note, however, that the government has a very important role in facilitating this process.

While preparing for the project, I decided to 'live' as if I was actually going to settle in Morocco. I therefore imagined that my partner found work in Morocco, and that I was transferring there with him. This seemed to me to be a situation that I can well imagine. I knew many women who immigrated to the Netherlands or elsewhere in order to be with their partners. Imagining myself as really moving to Morocco was important if I wanted to get the most from this project.

I took it upon myself to do everything to succeed in my civil integration in Morocco. Now, let me take you with me on this journey.

Start

My civil integration began the moment I boarded the airplane. Suddenly I found myself in a strange country. People spoke either Arabic or French, and I could neither speak nor understand either language. I felt so out of place. I almost did not dare to order a cup of tea and cookies from the stewardess. When I finally did it, it was with a lot of effort. When I realized that such a simple thing cost me a lot of effort, I wondered how it would be further on. The feeling of helplessness and discouragement began to creep into my blood.

Before me sat a woman whom I thought was Moroccan, with a child. After a while, I heard the child speak in Dutch; and it sounded like music to my ears! There is someone on the plane to Morocco who speaks my language! She even comes from Marrakech (where we were going) and was going there with her daughter for a vacation. I tried to get as much information on her city as I could, since I was going to 'immigrate' there. She seemed to be very friendly; and I was tempted to ask her the contact information of her family in Marrakech, so that I would have some social contact in my new city. But I thought that it would not be proper; so, I did not do it. Once in Marrakech, I regretted not having done so.

We stayed in a hotel in the centre of the old city, near the famous Djemaa el Fna. After settling in our rooms, I went out with a couple of other members of our group to get acquainted with the vicinity. I had a lot of impressions, especially regarding how different things were from that in the Netherlands. For example, it was a special art to cross a street safely. In the midst of all the commotion and the many impressions, I noted where important places were, e.g., a bank, an internet café. I had never had a big need to enter an internet café. Now, for me, it was a link with my family in the Netherlands (whom I missed a lot). Strange, but I missed my family a lot, even though I had just arrived in Morocco. Soon, I found myself in an internet café, and I quickly sent a message to my family. It took time to get used to the slow internet connection. But I really had a problem that the letters in the keyboard were arranged differently—my touch-typing ability was totally useless here.

For me, there was no problem sleeping during the first night. I was quite tired from the travel and the many first impressions. It felt as if I had just fallen asleep when I was awakened by a loud call to prayer from the nearby mosque. It seemed as if the call to prayer came from next door. I came to realize that religion and beliefs—in this case Islam—was so much a part of life in Morocco that it penetrates you, just like the call to prayer at four a.m. that woke me up. In the Netherlands, beliefs and religion are more personal and private matters. I wonder if I was awoken at four a.m. every day if I would eventually start praying. This was a foolish thought since the call to prayer did not wake me up on subsequent nights. I do not know why. Could it be that I had taken the call to prayer as something normal in this country, and that I no longer noticed it?

Intake, First Lessons
The next day, Tuesday, May 8, we were to leave at eight a.m. We were to take our civil integration lessons in a village school about forty-five minutes from Marrakech. We were to have an intake interview. The letter was written in Arabic; so, I did not understand anything in it, except for the time of the appointment. I couldn't ask anybody to translate the letter for me. We were told to wait in a room until someone came for us. The sphere of the intake interview was very formal. There was a translator present. During the interview, I was very nervous, and I felt insecure. The Arabic language sounded so serious. Later, when I had learned some Arabic words, the language sounded more melodious. Funny what emotional meaning you can attach to a language that you do not know; and how this can change once you have learnt the language.

The intake interview was, for me, the worst moment of the program. I had never felt so insecure. I did not recognize myself at all. I have always been a self-confident woman, who knew very well what I wanted and what I am capable of. But at that moment, I could not explain clearly what I expected of my life in Morocco, since I did not know it myself! I did not only feel insecure, but also angry and frustrated. Think of it—I had a career in the Netherlands, and I had to leave it! I could not imagine how I could build a new career in Morocco. It seemed such a tall mountain that I needed to climb. Can I use the skills and knowledge that I had learned in the Netherlands, in this country? Am I able to again learn new things, given my age? Do I have energy for that? These were the questions and insecurities that flashed through my mind, and they made me so sad. So sad that I felt it as pain. If I really had to immigrate to Morocco because of my husband, I would have had a terrible quarrel with him.

For a moment, I had to remind myself that this was just a project; that I could always stop with pretending that I would really be transferring to Morocco. I decided to go on pretending. I wanted to understand the process of civil integration, not only on an intellectual level, but also the emotions that went along with it.

Twenty-four years earlier—when I first arrived in the Netherlands—I did not feel the same insecurities that I felt in Morocco. I was young then, having just finished studying. For me, my life was still a big adventure, waiting for what would come my way. In a sense, I was then at the start of my career. But at the time of this project, I was already fifty-years-old, with a whole career path behind me, one for which I had worked very hard for. And I needed to leave all this! The feeling that went with this thought was unbearable! It did not feel like an adventure (unlike twenty-four years ago), but more a feeling of insecurity, fear, sadness and frustration.

In the afternoon, we had a lesson about the Moroccan society, in Dutch. I gradually grew more relaxed. It seemed as if a new world was gradually opening for me. The lesson was short; and during the lesson, I tried to learn as much as possible about the country. I was mainly interested in women. In the Netherlands, I worked a lot with women, and I was looking for possibilities to continue working with women. This was something concrete that I can focus on, next to learning Arabic. I had a concrete goal, and it felt good! From this, I was able to get so much energy to face the challenge of civil integration in the coming days.

Maria

The next day something happened that gave an important twist to my civil integration process. At breakfast, a Moroccan woman asked nicely if I liked the food. I answered her slowly in English. It turned out that the woman's English was rather good. I sat down beside her and introduced myself. When she heard my name, she said that she would never forget me. Our names were similar: I was Maya, and she was Maria. I then told her that Maria was my official Christian name, and that Maya was a nickname. She was so happy to hear this, as if a bond connected us. We talked. I told her about the objective of our trip to Morocco and that I was mainly interested in meeting women. She became enthusiastic and said that she could introduce me to a couple of women. Later that day she came back to our hotel with four other women. Two of them often came to visit me in the succeeding days of my stay. They helped me with my assignment 'orientation with society'. They also helped me practice some Arabic words. In exchange, I taught them some English words. It turned out that Maria was an entrepreneur and had a travel agency. I was able to have my practicum in her company. Maria was, just like me, the mother of a teenager. We talked a lot about raising children, especially about the generation gap and the fast-changing culture of Morocco; and what consequences these had for raising children. My meeting with women gave me the feeling that I could make it in Morocco. I became more motivated to learn the Arabic language. If I had stayed longer in Morocco,

I would have certainly started a women's group. And if I was to really settle in Morocco, I would have surely taken a course.

An important component of our civil integration was, naturally, learning the Arabic language. Our teacher was very competent and patient. He spoke only Arabic, but he was able to teach us the language. I was exhausted after a morning's language lesson. But I actually enjoyed the lessons. It was as if a whole world was opening up for me. Great!

As an expert-through-experience in the area of civil integration, I still learned a lot from the project. It was a very concentrated experience, such that things that had to do with civil integration were put in sharp focus. To my fellow non-native-born Dutch, I would like to say the following: Go for it, embrace your new environment, and follow your dreams. And while you are at it, enjoy all that is new in your life. Your civil integration in the Netherlands is in your hands and keep it so.

From my policy-making role as a city councillor, I want to point out the following:

- civil integration is more than learning the language. The role of the receiving society is just as important for a successful civil integration process. A social network that caters to the interests of the newcomer is crucial in the process of civil integration.

- the newcomers' education, work experience and interests are important sources of inspiration for the newcomer for their intrinsic motivation for civil integration to come out. Telling newcomers to put their ambitions on hold and first just learn the language, can be deadly for their motivation.

Chapter 12
Opstap: A Child's Learning Begins at Home

'Parents' participation is key in a child's education'

Ayse, a Turkish migrant to the Netherlands, had brought her 6-year-old son Mehmet to school in the morning; and then walked over to the teacher to talk about volunteering for the school's sports day the following week. Six months earlier, Ayse would never have lingered after bringing Mehmet; she would hurry away in order to avoid talking with the teacher. The ***Opstap*** program, which they participated in, had changed that and many other things.

Six months earlier, I had approached Ayse and her husband and asked if they would like to participate in the ***Opstap*** Program together with their son Mehmet. They had agreed. Since then, they were visited regularly by a *buurtmoeder* (a para-professional woman who helped program participants), and they received children's books, play materials and exercises for them to do with Mehmet. It took getting used to: role playing with the *buurtmoeder*, reading books to Mehmet, playing with and doing exercises with Mehmet, and all this with a lot of patience. The *buurtmoeder* showed her how to do it and taught her to be patient when Mehmet was distracted or inattentive. In addition to the daily sessions with Mehmet, every two weeks Ayse would attend a meeting with other participating mothers to discuss topics related to child-rearing. In one session, she learned that it was better to praise children when they do something well, instead of merely scolding them when they do something wrong. She also learned that her participation in school activities would benefit their child.

Mehmet looks forward to his daily *Opstap* sessions with his mother. He has changed from being a shy and reluctant child, to one who looks forward to going to school.

My first paid job in the Netherlands was as program coordinator of the *Opstap* program. *Opstap* is an early childhood home-based intervention program designed to help children of migrant parents do better in Dutch schools. Dutch families living in low social economic conditions (such as unemployment and low educational level) also participated in the program. In a period of two years, when the child is from four to six years old, a *buurtmoeder* visits the family every week. She then brings with her the exercises and children's book for the following week. The *buurtmoeder* would then explain to the parent (in most cases the mother) the activities the parents can do with their child for the coming week. She does this mainly by role playing, the *buurtmoeder* acting as if she was the mother, and the mother acting as if she was the child. The materials are in the mother language of the parents. So, a Turkish family, for example, gets materials in the Turkish language. The *buurtmoeder* is also a woman with similar migrant background as the parents. So, Turkish families are visited by a Turkish *buurtmoeder*. The idea behind this is to let migrant parents' experience that they can still help their young child in her/his development and school learning, even if they do not speak the Dutch language well.

My work as a program coordinator of the *Opstap* project—which I did for almost nine years—gave me a deeper understanding of the Dutch educational system. As program coordinator, I had regular consultations with the schoolteachers of the participating children, with the community child health workers, with the social workers of the community centres and other local institutions involved in child development, such as local libraries.

Elementary education, called basic education in the Netherlands, is mainly aimed at preparing the child (from four to twelve years old) for further vocational, professional or academic learning. Elementary school children learn the basic elements necessary for learning, such as language (reading, writing, speaking and comprehension), arithmetic, how to look for information and process it as a basis to form one's opinion, and developing a positive attitude towards learning. All these elements are factored in in the *Opstap* program. Reading a book to one's child is, for example, a regular activity in the *Opstap* program. This helps increase the vocabulary of the child, and also stimulates the child to read books in later years. Also, when parents read books to their young child, the child experiences this as a positive learning experience. This contributes to developing a positive attitude towards learning.

Play also has an important place in the learning process of young children. Early education in the Netherlands puts emphasis on learning through play. This helps instil in the children that learning is fun. When learning is fun, children love to learn and therefore will learn better. A lot of exercises in the *Opstap* program are actually acting-out and play activities. When parents do the exercises with their children, the children experience this as a positive and fun learning experience. This too contributes to developing a positive attitude towards learning.

The Dutch educational system gives high importance to parental involvement. It is believed that children learn better in school if their parents show interest and are involved in the school activities of their children. By participating in the *Opstap* program, migrant parents are encouraged to also be involved in the school activities of their children, like Ayse who volunteered for the school sports day of her child Mehmet.

When I started to work as program coordinator of the *Opstap* program in October 1993, Elena was then four years old. I did all the exercises in the program with her, as a way to prepare the training program for the *buurtmoeders* and the group sessions with the mothers. By doing the exercises myself with my own child I experienced how it is to do all the exercises and play activities. I then understood how frustrating it could also be to parents if their children were not so cooperative. Aside from just going through the instructions of the exercises and activities, also included was a session on how to deal with situations when children are less cooperative, or are slow in doing the exercises, etc. In any case, I would advise the parents not to force their children to do the exercises and activities with them, as it is important that doing those exercises and activities should be a positive experience for their children. On the other hand, I would also tell the parents that I understand them when they sometimes get frustrated and angry with their children, since I myself had experienced it too.

Reading a book to one's child or doing acting-out and play activities with their children are not so common for migrant parents to do. At the start of the program, most participating mothers feel therefore awkward doing all the activities of the program. During the latter part of the program though, most mothers feel comfortable reading a book and playing with their children.

An important part of the program was the group sessions of

the participating mothers. These were held every two weeks and took place either in the community centres or in their children's schools. During these group sessions, the mothers had a chance to share their experiences in doing the activities of the program with their children. In the course of the program period, the mothers developed a certain level of trust with each other such that they would also bring up their dilemmas and difficulties in the upbringing of their children during the group sessions. They would then give each other tips how to deal with these dilemmas and difficulties. As program coordinator it was my role to ensure that mothers maintained their respect for each other, that there were no judgmental comments made to each other, and that the mothers would realize that each situation is different and needs a different approach and that one approach is not necessarily better than the other. In so doing I was able to maintain the feeling of safety and security of all the participants during the group sessions.

During the group sessions the mothers would also get information about the various institutions which were relevant for the growth and development of their children, such as the Public Health Care Services (**GGD**), the public library, the children's activities in the community centres, etc. Informing the parents about these institutions and services stimulated them to make more optimal use of these services. This will then contribute to their child's healthy growth and development.

During the group sessions we also discussed various topics pertaining to child-rearing. One such topic, which was an important underlying principle of the program, was developing a positive-responsive approach towards our children. Many parents tend to focus on the negative behaviour of children, such as not listening, being disobedient, making a mess of the room with their toys, etc. From a positive-responsive approach parents are encouraged to give more attention to the positive things' children do. So, instead of scolding them when they do not put away their toys after playing, an alternative approach is saying something positive when they do put away their toys after playing, or even better put the toys away together with them making it as some kind of a play. Other topics which were also discussed during the group sessions were about punishment and reward—alternative forms of punishment which were not harmful for the children and reflecting on one's purpose of punishing one's children; about values which parents find important in the upbringing of their children; how to help children develop self-confidence; setting up rules and limits with children, about the growth and development of children, etc. While I facilitated these group sessions, I also learnt a lot from the experiences the mothers shared during those group sessions.

 While the ***Opstap*** program was mainly developed to help the child learn better in school, I also saw a lot of benefits it had for the mothers. For one, the mothers got a better idea about what their children were already capable (or not yet capable) of doing. With this insight they were in a better position to support their children in their development by doing activities which were more appropriate to their children. Mothers also became more interested in what their children were doing in school. Many participating mothers did not just drop off their children to school but started to make time to also walk into their children's classroom, look at the schoolwork of their children and talk to the teacher. During the teacher-parent consultations after every grading period, the mothers also understood their children's school report better, wherein a fruitful discussion ensued between parents and teachers on the steps to help the child further in his/her school learning and development. All these contributed to the mothers developing more self-confidence in the upbringing of their children. I also noticed that this self-confidence went further to a more general self-confidence, such that some mothers also started to undertake activities for themselves like taking Dutch lessons, taking a course or actively looking for a part-time job. Many of the *buurtmoeders* of the program were former participants of the program.

After two years, at the end of the program, we would organize a festive activity in which the participating children would get their *Opstap* diploma. Many times, we would organize these closing activities in the city's Cultural Centre, and I would marvel at the enthusiastic faces of the many children and their mothers who are entering the Cultural Centre for the first time.

I look back to those years as very fulfilling years. It warmed my heart to see so many children getting that positive support from their parents such that they may grow in a warm and stimulating environment. It also warmed my heart to see so many women develop in their role as mothers, but also as women, and as persons.

Years later, I would sometimes have chance encounters with participating mothers of the *Opstap* program. They would then tell me how happy and proud they are of what their children have achieved and would tell me that this is because of the *Opstap* program and would thank me for it. I would then tell them, "You did it yourself."

Chapter 13
A Paradox of Life

Understanding refugees.

On November 3, 2010, I posted the following on my Facebook page, in Dutch:

"The conversation I had yesterday with a refugee still kept lingering in my mind. She was a thirty-six--year-old Ethiopian woman who fled to the Netherlands when she was eighteen years of age. She however got her refugee status only in 2007. When I asked her what she wants to achieve in life, she could not answer this question. She told me that when she came to the Netherlands eighteen years ago, she was full of plans of what to learn and what to do with her life. But since she did not have a status as a refugee, she was prohibited to do anything by the Dutch government, such as learning the language and studying for a vocation. So, she spent half of her life mostly in the refugee centre, doing nothing but wait for the decision on her asylum application! Now, after so many years of not being allowed to do anything, she no longer knows what she wants to achieve in life. She fled from a war to be able to survive. But the country that she hoped could save her, where she hoped to build a new future, somehow broke her. What a paradox of life!"

I started working for the Council for Refugees (***Vluchtelingenwerk***) in April 2002, when I decided to make a shift in my career after having worked for almost nine years with an institution for social work and welfare in the city where I live. I worked as head of the integration department and had twelve social workers under my supervision. Our role was to give social guidance to refugees who had already been granted stay permits. Later, and up to the present, I work as project leader of various programs aimed at helping refugees integrate well in Dutch society. In my work I did not really have contact with refugees on a daily basis. But as the head of our department for integration then, I would regularly intervene if our social workers were having difficulties in their dealings with the refugees they were assisting. Once, one of our social workers asked me to intervene because her client behaved quite aggressively and was very angry. I then talked to this refugee and asked what the reason was for his anger. I found out that this refugee was very frustrated with the Dutch government authorities which he found very bureaucratic. I stayed calm and explained patiently to him the rules. He also became calm and told me "I cannot be angry with you. You remind me of my mother." I was actually quite amused with what he said.

With my present task as project leader for integration and participation my contact with refugees is also not on a daily basis. In the process of designing workshops and courses for refugees on a wide range of topics about the Dutch society, I would give the first try out of these workshops and courses to groups of refugees. Since many of them have not yet mastered the Dutch language, I would ask a refugee (a former client of V*luchtelingenwerk*) who had lived longer in the Netherlands to translate during these workshops and courses. It inspires me to see many of them getting more and more active in Dutch society.

After having worked for almost nine years as program coordinator of ***Opstap***, a parenting program for mothers with young children in the various disadvantaged communities in Tilburg, I thought I had already seen the worst possible problems people and families may have. But during my work with *Vluchtelingenwerk* I realized that the situation of many refugees was far worse.

Refugees had left their respective countries without any or with very little preparation. They had to flee hurriedly to escape the dangers of war. They therefore have very few things with them, only the very basic such as clothes and some money. Many of them were not able to bring their school diplomas with them, only to realize that they would be needing these once they had acquired a stay permit in their new host country in order to qualify for jobs. The Netherlands is such a 'paper country'—you need to have documents for almost anything you do. Many of them are also not able to travel together as a family. It is usually the man who first travels to their final destination, like the Netherlands, and the wife and children stay behind in refugee camps in the region. Once the man gets his stay permit, meaning that his application for asylum has been granted, he then starts the process of family reunification so that his wife and children can follow him to the Netherlands. The asylum application process takes several months, in many cases even several years. And the ensuing process of family reunification also takes several months, sometimes even more than a year. So, you could just imagine how long the family had been living in uncertainty about their future and separated from each other. I could not find the right words to describe the emotional burden this situation has caused the refugees. But I often hear from our volunteer's giving guidance to these refugees that many refugees begin to show signs of depression after they have been reunited with their family. It is like they have put aside all their feelings during the whole process of asylum application and family reunification, and all these feelings and emotions have burst open at the end of the process, like a dam which has burst its banks.

When one has just arrived in the Netherlands it is of course understandable that one is not knowledgeable about the systems of this country, such as health care, education, welfare subsidies, matters regarding taxes and income, etc. Getting sufficient knowledge on these matters take time, especially because one does not yet speak nor understand the Dutch language. Most traditional migrants (i.e., non-refugees) have quite a big network of family members and friends who have already lived for quite a long time in the Netherlands. Their network of family members and friends could then assist them in the first few years of their new life in the Netherlands. In contrast, however, most refugees do not have this network. This makes it extra difficult for them to establish their new life in the Netherlands, due to many years of living in uncertainty whether or not their application for asylum will be granted.

Having left their respective countries hurriedly and having no network of family and friends, many of the refugees also do not have any financial resources when they come to the Netherlands. Thanks to the Dutch welfare state, they do receive social benefits from the Dutch government for their daily subsistence the moment their asylum status is granted. To be able to furnish their house they also receive a loan from the Dutch government specific for this purpose. Next to this they could also get a loan from the Dutch government to be able to take the required Dutch language lessons. So, refugees do not only have a lot of catching up to do to be able to settle and get on with their lives in the Netherlands, but they also start with their new life in the Netherlands with debts. It is therefore not surprising that many refugees live in poverty. For refugees with a good life in their country of origin this is extra painful. During a group session with some Syrian women refugees, they told me that it breaks their heart that they are not able to provide their children with the things they used to provide them. They will have to do with second hand clothes and stuff. Personally, I think there is nothing wrong with using second hand stuff, this is good for the environment. But if this is not your own choice, then it is painful.

Not all asylum seekers are granted an asylum status. And some could have their asylum status revoked or not renewed. In this last case, this has something to do with the type of asylum status one gets, the so-called categorical protection. This kind of asylum is then not granted on the basis of individual merit but is given to a group of refugees coming from a country clearly in war. A disadvantage of having this type of status is that it can be revoked or not renewed once the Dutch government thinks that the war in that specific country is already over. So, with this line of reasoning, the Dutch government finds it responsible and safe to send these refugees back to these countries. But what the Dutch government fails to see is that these refugees have already started their new life in the Netherlands. So, uprooting them again from their new found life is really very harsh. And this is extra hard if there are children involved. Many children of these refugees came to the Netherlands at a very young age or were even born in the Netherlands. So, these children have not known any other country but the Netherlands. Imagine a child, who had been going to a Dutch school, had made a lot of friends at school and in her neighbourhood, and behaves like any other Dutch child—and is suddenly sent back to Afghanistan, a country she has never known. And life in Afghanistan is far different from life in the Netherlands. How could you do such a thing to a child? I find this simply cruel! Recently the Dutch government came to an agreement to implement amnesty to children refugees and their parents. About 600 children (and their parents) could avail of this amnesty. This was a result of the many protests and appeals coming from the Dutch public, including many school children. This is a beacon of hope we should cherish.

The refugees did not choose to leave their country, they had to flee. And in doing so, they had to practically leave everything behind, and have to start life anew. Comments in the media about refugees, that they are here to profit from the welfare state in the Netherlands, could really make my blood boil in anger and frustration. It is so sad that a lot of people do not realize and understand how it is to be a refugee. *Vluchtelingenwerk*, the foundation where I work, also holds activities stimulating interaction between refugees and the local Dutch people where they live. With these activities we hope to increase the understanding of people towards refugees. But what we are doing is just actually a 'small drop on a hot iron plate'. I look forward to the day when refugees would really be welcomed in this country, so they may pick up the lost years of their life faster and are able to participate and contribute to their new country, the Netherlands. I believe that refugees have a lot to offer (knowledge, skills, insights, and qualities), things which could be very useful for the Netherlands and the Dutch society.

Chapter 14
The Walk of the World

'The last ten kilometres are the hardest.'

In July 2010, I was watching on television the entry of the walkers of the Four Day Marches in Nijmegen 2010. Out of enthusiasm, I said out loud, "I would like to do that next year".

My daughter Elena replied promptly, "You cannot just do that, you know. You really have to train for that."

"I will," I answered her automatically while I continued watching the news about it. This was more or less the start of my interest for the walking sports.

A year later, in 2011, I was no longer watching the entry of the walkers of the Four Day Marches in Nijmegen on television; I myself was in it, walking the last metres to the 'Finish' of the 95th Four Day Marches in Nijmegen.

I had joined for the first time the Four Day Marches in Nijmegen, also known as 'The Walk of the World'. I walked four times forty kilometres, making one hundred and sixty kilometres in four days! It was a very special experience. What I thought was a pure physical endeavour, turned out to be more than that. Those four days demanded from me not only physical exertion but also mental and spiritual exertion and strength as well. I have never listened so much to my body as during those four days. I have never coordinated my body, mind and spirit so much as in those four days. Everything in me worked only towards that one objective, and that was to reach the 'Finish' on the fourth day.

Unexpectedly I got something extra special on those days. Every day I spent about ten hours (including the rests in-between) to make those kilometres. You can just imagine how much time I had to reflect about so many things, to shut me off from life's daily routine and issues of the day, to just listen to my inner self, without the stress from having to meet deadlines, and not having to go with the rush of these modern times.

The Four Day March's route went through a different set of villages around Nijmegen every day. The people of the villages had festivities to greet the walkers as they passed by. Each day of the Four Day March was special, and each had its own character.

On the first day (July 19) I was very impressed with the sphere of the whole event. I was especially impressed with the enormous unity of people from all walks of life: between the elderly and the youth, between the city people and the people living in the countryside, between the sporting and not-so-sporting people. There were children and adults offering candies, cookies and fruit to walkers passing by people along the road who were cheering the walkers and wishing them success, people who were offering their toilets for free use to the walkers, and people who were distributing drinking water to walkers. "It would be great if this unity will always be present in our society", I thought to myself. "It was very special to have experienced this unity."

At about the last ten kilometres, the pain in my feet started to dominate my senses. Because of the pain, you start asking yourself a lot of philosophical questions like: "Why did I participate in this event?", "What am I doing this for?" I tried to think of answers to these questions. Is it because my daughters Ligaya and Elena are proud of me, and I want to keep it that way? Is it because my husband Carlo assumes that I will get to the

'Finish' on the 4th day? Is it because my colleague Mirjam wrote in her encouragement message to me that she never doubts, not for one moment, my capacity for perseverance? Is it because I did not want the foundation, I was raising funds for during this event, to miss their sponsor money? I even thought about the terrible drought in the Horn of Africa and how people there had to walk hundreds of kilometres without any food or water, on their bare feet, just to survive. The news about it was on TV just before I left for Nijmegen, and it had touched me deeply. And here I was complaining about my painful feet, while I was well-equipped with a good pair of walking shoes, and food and drink for on the way. None of these answers could make me forget about the pain in my feet. So, I finally just said to myself: "Hey, stop complaining, just continue walking!"

Day 2 (July 20) was for me a day of philosophizing and self-reflection, not because of the pain I was feeling in my feet, but from the inner peace I felt that day. At the start of the day, I was still a bit worried that I would not sustain the day's walk. I was still sleepy and tired, and I dreamt of just staying in bed the whole day. "This is a bad way to start," I thought. But my adrenaline seemed to have worked quite fast, after just a few minutes of walking I started to feel okay, and I continued to feel great for most of the walk. A big part of the route was quiet and peaceful, or did it seem only quiet and peaceful because I was so absorbed with my own thoughts? It does not really matter, but I really enjoyed the inner peace I was experiencing. I thought about what Elena told me two days ago when I told her that I was a bit worried that I wouldn't make all those four days of walking.

"Oh, do not worry mom, you have nothing to worry about; you are capable of achieving everything. You always are."

That was really sweet of her to assure me that way, but

nobody is capable of achieving everything, I thought then to myself. But actually, she had a point! If you really want something, then you can really do it. For as long as you are prepared to really work hard for it. For as long as you are prepared to accept that it hurts every now and then, and despite the pain would still continue and persevere anyway. For as long as you are prepared to seek support and encouragement from your environment and accept it wholeheartedly. For as long as you are prepared to take good care of yourself, physically, mentally, emotionally and spiritually. And for as long as you are prepared to also enjoy your travel towards your goal. When I thought about all these, then I knew for sure that I will succeed in this Four Day March in Nijmegen. The last ten kilometres were, just as the first day, also the hardest for me this time. It felt as if there was no end to these last kilometres. But this time I did not think anymore of the hardship of people in the Horn of Africa, but I just allowed myself to enjoy the cheers and encouragement from the people along the road.

Day 3 (July 21) was for me a day of the 'automatic pilot' in me. When my alarm clock went off at 4 am that morning, I just got out of bed without complaining and started with my daily 'morning ritual': covered the painful and sensitive parts of my feet with plasters for blisters, lubricated the soles of my feet with a thick layer of foot cream, ate breakfast even though my stomach was not yet really awake, packed sandwiches, water and energy drink in my backpack, and set off for the start. There was no philosophizing that day, I just allowed myself to enjoy the reception people made in every town and village we passed by, and to enjoy the quiet route in-between the towns and villages. In some of those quiet moments some of the walkers tried to crack jokes and sang songs, as their way of cheering us up. And I also just joined them in laughter. It felt as if this day was just a day to get through with, and just do what needed to be done. Then I came to the last ten kilometres, which were always the heaviest part for me. A hilly part, the so-called Seven Hills, was part of these last ten kilometres. While approaching this part of the route I heard a lot of complaining from the other walkers about how difficult this route was. But to my surprise I found it very pleasant because with the alternating uphill and downhill walking, the pressure points on my feet kept changing, and this had a soothing effect on my feet. In contrast to what I had heard earlier, I had a positive experience with this supposedly difficult part of the route. Or was I just the hopeless optimist, who always saw the positive side of things?

Day 4 (July 22) was the day of victory, walking through the Via Gladiola towards the 'Finish'. This was the sphere of the whole day. It was as if everybody had only one goal, and that was to make it to the 'Finish'. I no longer heard any complaints from my fellow walkers, people just continued walking. Some of the walkers were limping from the pain in their feet. But most of the walkers, including myself, continued to walk 'normally' as if they did not feel pain in their feet. I knew too well that most of them, just like me, also had pain in their feet. It really felt like I was a 'tough guy'—still walking straight and even briskly despite the pain in my feet. I guess it was on this 4-day walking event that I experienced for the first time how it is to feel like a 'tough guy'. And it is quite a good feeling actually.

Walking through the Via Gladiola was a very special experience. It felt as if 'I was coming home' after having fought an important battle, welcomed and cheered by thousands of people. The euphoria I felt was tremendous, my feet seemed to get wings. I knew that my family was waiting for me somewhere along the road. In these four days I really got a lot of support from them, they were with me all the time. I could not wait to see them. The street seemed so long. It is by the way also a really long street, the St. Anna Street in Nijmegen.

It really was a very nice feeling to finally see my family, waiting for me. Later that day Carlo reminded me of our family tradition to be always together when one of us has just made an important achievement, that we always shared these moments with each other. That is indeed true.

Then the last few metres still had to be made. And finally, the most beautiful banner of all was in sight, the **FINISH**.

Chapter 15
The Last Ten Kilometres are the Hardest

Reflections while preparing for the Night of the Refugee.

Whenever I told friends and acquaintances that I planned to walk in the **Night of the Refugee** (a fund-raising event, where you walk forty kilometres, starting at midnight), I often got the reaction: "That is quite a distance! Do you realize that?" Yes, I know that it is quite a distance, and that I should not underestimate it. I also know how it feels to walk this distance. Several years ago, in 2011, I walked the **Nijmegen Four Day Marches** of four times forty kilometres. I was then a bit younger, and I also did not take medication then that would make me feel tired. So, I found it exciting to again walk forty kilometres.

From April 28 to May 3, 2018, I walked the first six stages of the **Pieterpad**—a total of one hundred and eleven kilometres. (The Pieterpad has a total of twenty-six stages.) Because I did this partly in preparation for the Night of the Refugee, I thought about the refugees while walking. I thought about the refugees especially on Tuesday when I had to walk the whole day in the rain. And I realized that one could not possibly know how it is to flee on foot for your life for endless kilometres, hoping for a safer and better future. While I had to walk through the cold, wind and rain, I knew that at the end of that stage, there was a warm bed in a Bed and Breakfast waiting for me. But do refugees have that while they were on the run? They only had hope… hope that they will end up well somewhere. I know that I could not offer hope for these refugees. But by participating in the Night of the Refugee, I want to contribute to giving refugees a dry and warm bed, clean water and some food. No, not a Bed and Breakfast, but simply the basic requirements for a humane and decent initial shelter.

When I think about the Nijmegen Four Day Marches of several years before, I remember that I found the last ten kilometres the heaviest, every day. My feet hurt, my legs were tired, my hands were numb and swollen, and my arms were weak because they had been passively hanging from my body all day. You may say that the last ten kilometres should be an easy additional distance to walk. After all, I had already walked a longer distance, and the end is not that far away anymore. But because your whole body hurts and you are tired, the last ten kilometres seem endless. Yes, I still remember it quite well: the last ten kilometres are the hardest.

When I think of the refugees, I can compare the last ten kilometres to when they finally obtain their permits to stay. The worst is over, they would think. The end cannot be that far away anymore—a new life in the Netherlands. But they are already physically, mentally, emotionally and psychologically exhausted from their journey up to that point. But many of them must also live in uncertainty of whether they will succeed in bringing over their families. Then they also need to learn the Dutch language, adapt to new practices and norms, and deal with the expectation of people that they swiftly adapt to the Dutch society, etc. A new life in the Netherlands—the 'Finish'—seems to be not too far away; but at the same time, it feels like it is beyond their reach. This could still break them.

By walking the Night of the Refugee, I not only wanted to

raise funds for a decent initial shelter for refugees worldwide, but I also wanted to support the refugees already in the Netherlands who are busy with their 'last ten kilometres and to let them see that there are enough people in the Netherlands who want to grant them a new life here. To tell them: "go on, keep on going, the 'Finish' is in sight."

On June 16 to 17, 2018, I walked forty kilometres, from Rotterdam to Den Haag, during the Night of the Refugee.

Chapter 16
Musings on my Long-Distance Walks

'Conversations with my soul'

When I told some friends that I will walk the Pieterpad, many were surprised to hear that I would be doing this alone. "You're a tough one. Is that not scary, walking through places you've never been before, walking through forests, ALONE?", my friends would exclaim.

"Now that you say that I am beginning to be afraid", I would jokingly answer back. But honestly, I do find it a bit scary. But it is definitely much less scary than parachute jumping. And one important character trait I have is that I do not want to be withheld by fear. So, that feeling of fear would just flash in a split second through my mind.

What is the Pieterpad? The **Pieterpad** is a long-distance walking route in the Netherlands, starting from **Pieter**buren up north in Groningen, and ends at St. **Pieter**sberg down south in Maastricht. One can also walk it from south to north. It has a total distance of four hundred and ninety-eight kilometres, divided into twenty-six stages. The route passes by small villages, goes through forests, open fields and natural reserves. As of writing this article I have already finished seventeen stages covering a total of three hundred and fifteen kilometres.

What made me want to walk the Pieterpad? Well, I heard that the route passes through very beautiful natural landscapes.

Walking the Pieterpad is one way of seeing more of the Netherlands, especially places where I would not have gone to, such as small remote villages and natural reserves and forests. Another reason for me to want to walk the Pieterpad is that I see this as a way to prepare for a longer walking challenge, the **Camino de Santiago de Compostela**. I also want to walk this on my own, alone, and am thinking of doing the classical French route which covers a total of more than seven hundred kilometres. Unlike the Pieterpad which I will be walking in stages spread over two years (I started in 2018 and hope to finish sometime in 2020 but due to the Corona pandemic I was not able to walk in 2020.) I am planning to walk the Camino de Santiago continuously for a period of about thirty-five days. I hope that I can do this sometime in 2022. So actually, walking the Pieterpad is in my case connected to a bigger challenge of walking the Camino de Santiago—the Pieterpad paving the way for a bigger challenge, making the way towards achieving it easier. In reflection, this is actually also a nice metaphor for life. If you want to achieve something, you can work your way towards that goal by doing things, taking (smaller) steps which would bring you closer to that goal, steps which could pave the way towards that goal and make the way towards that goal easier for you to take. And at the same time, you take pleasure in taking those smaller steps, as those smaller steps also have their own beauty by itself.

In the early morning, while still in bed, before I started out to walk the first stage of the Pieterpad, a lot of thoughts came to my mind, thoughts connected to long distance walking which were actually interesting metaphors for life. In long distance walking, your goal (your destination) is actually already there, further down the road. You only need to find it, walk towards it.

In your journey towards it, you will be needing your inner compass (your judgment about which turns to make), but also other people who can show you the way, or help you clear the obstacles along the road. And in the meantime, you can also enjoy your journey, for there are lots of things to see and to experience along the road towards your destination, your goal. These were the thoughts I had with me when I started out with my Pieterpad adventure.

I walked the first two stages of the Pieterpad with Ligaya. This served as some kind of a nudge to help me get started. I especially enjoyed our conversations. In the succeeding stages I walked alone. Most of the time I was actually alone, walking through open fields, through forests and through small villages. Every now and then I would encounter other walkers going the opposite direction or in the same direction as I was but who walked at a faster pace.

Walking alone was by itself a special experience. I could reflect on a lot of things, mostly about life. It allowed me to hear my thoughts loud and clear. It was actually like I was conversing with my soul. I had with me a notebook which I got from Elena the previous Christmas. Before going to sleep in my Bed & Breakfast after every stage, I would find time to scribble my thoughts quickly in my notebook. I would like to share these thoughts with you here.

The route from Zuidlaren to Rolde on the fourth day was really very beautiful. I walked through a natural reserve in Drenthe, and also through the lovely Balloerveld. It was a pity that the flower field was not yet in full bloom, but nevertheless it was very lovely. The weather forecast that day was rain for the whole day. And it really did rain, the whole day! When I started off that morning with my walk, I made a decision that I will really enjoy the landscape despite the rain. It did not only rain the whole day, but there was also a lot of wind, especially in the afternoon. So, I really was feeling very cold. It was therefore a big challenge for me to still enjoy the landscape. I consciously focused my attention on all the beauty around me, and consciously made pictures to force myself to stop, look at the view, admire and enjoy it. Relating this to life, I realized that it is actually possible to focus on something positive, still see and recognize the good things happening in your life, even in the midst of your problems and discomfort. But this has to be a choice you need to make. It is a big challenge to do this, but it can be done. And this can help you through your problems and discomfort. Had I only focused on all my discomfort that day—the rain, wind, cold and the pain in my feet—then I would just have walked past the beautiful landscape, without seeing and enjoying it. What a missed opportunity it would have been!

Since it rained for several days, pathways were muddy. I also had to avoid puddles. I also walked through narrow foot paths, with weeds growing over them. I therefore had to focus on the ground, carefully paying attention to where I should put my feet while walking, to avoid stumbling or falling. Because of this I was not able to pay attention to my surroundings and have therefore missed a lot of possible nice views. This is a pity, but sometimes it is just how it is. Relating this to life, there are times when you need to also focus on your problems, to avoid stumbling or falling. And indeed, during these times you will miss a lot of good things happening in your surroundings. This is also part of life.

Sometimes I would walk long, straight stretches of asphalted or cemented roads. This is actually my least favourite part of my walks. The road being hard puts too much pressure on my feet, such that my feet would hurt. I prefer walking on rough tracks, and even much better on grass. They are kinder to my feet. Walking on long, straight stretches of road (mostly were asphalted or cemented) is also very discouraging. I would then just see how far it still is. I prefer walking on winding roads (they were mostly rough tracks). You then do not get to see how far you still have to walk, and while walking you are also doing a lot of manoeuvring—curving to the right, then to the left, climb over a fence, over a small bridge, etc. You are then less conscious of the distance you still have to cover, and before you know it you have already reached your destination. Relating this to life, focusing always on the things you must do (like walking that long stretch of road) could be discouraging and could cause too much pressure on you. While doing little things along the way could serve as a good diversion helping you get through life.

On one of those days, a father and his son who were walking in the same direction as I was overtook me. I noticed that I had the tendency to look at where they were going, which turn they made, and to keep up my pace with them, afraid of being left behind. After a while of doing this, I realized that I actually started to doubt my own judgment, whether I understood well the instructions in my guide book. This did not feel good, so I decided to go back to simply trusting myself again and follow the route as I know it from my guide book and from the signs along the way. Trusting yourself is a choice you have to make.

In all those days of long distance walking I realized that your body, and especially your feet, are actually your most loyal companion. Time and again, my body was able to recover well enough such that I could again proceed with my walk the following day. It felt as if my body was aware of what I was trying to achieve and was with me in this endeavour. Listening well to your body and giving it time to recover is therefore very important. Take good care of your body, it is your most loyal companion, you need it to bring you to the place where you want to be.

And lastly, I experienced that water actually has a healing effect on your body. After having taken a shower, after every long walk, a lot of pain disappears from my body, as if the water washed them all away, and the process of recovering and healing of my body has started.

Chapter 17
A Fair Secret

A fair can be a photo album of memories.

It is no secret that the Tilburg Summer Fair is the city's biggest 'happening'. The hundreds of thousands of people laughing and screaming through the fair grounds are proof of that. But what people do not know, is that the fair has many secrets—secrets that reside in the hearts of the people who walk the fair grounds. Take a good look in the eyes of these people. Here is one such secret in the making...

Every year, in July, Tilburg closes four and a half kilometres of city streets in the city centre (plus some city squares) and fills them with rides, booths etc. for its Summer Fair, in a tradition that started four hundred and fifty years ago.

It is July 2047. Carol prepares to go to the Fair. She is going to the Fair, as she has for years. This year, though, she will have to go alone. Her husband, Henry, died during the past winter. Carol and Henry have two daughters, and four grandchildren. Both daughters now live abroad, with their families. When they still lived in the Netherlands, they would always come with their children to Tilburg during the Fair. The Tilburg Summer Fair had become a family tradition. For as long as they can remember, there was always a Tilburg Summer Fair. When both their daughters moved abroad, the Fair served for Carol and Henry as a kind of photobook, where they brought out their memories every year.

Carol got off the bus at the Besterdplein, at the edge of the Fair on the north side of the Centrum. With her walker, she walked slowly through the Fair, and the beginning of her 'photobook'. At the bumper-cars, she saw her youngest daughter at the steering wheel, steering the car with Henry. Her eldest daughter sat proudly in another bumper car; very proud that she was allowed to do so by herself. And Carol rode in still another bumper car. They tried to bump each other's cars and laughed with each bump.

Further on were the airplanes that you could raise or lower by pushing or pulling a lever. She saw her grandchildren laughing and waving, while on their airplanes. Tess, the youngest of her eldest daughter had no idea how to steer the plane, but she enjoyed the ride as much as the others. Her daughter ran after Tess' airplane, trying to tell her how she could steer her plane, but without success. Carol saw herself looking at her two daughters, who were watching their children with excitement and happiness. "Oh, my daughters have grown up" she thought, her heart full of joy at seeing her daughters as mothers.

The ponies were always the favourite of her youngest, and later also of her daughter (Carol's granddaughter). She can still hear her daughter saying "Mama, may I have a ride on the pony?"

And later, her granddaughter would always say, "One more time, please?"

She stopped by the Catapult, to see how two boys will be flung by it. Her daughters were teenagers when the Catapult first came to Tilburg. It was quite a spectacle, and her daughters just had to try it out. She heard her daughters screaming and laughing as they were flung by the Catapult up and down. She had never dared to try out the high and fast rides. Her youngest daughter always teased her for being such a sissy. Each year, she attempted to get her to try out one of these rides.

Ah! There is the banana game, smiled Carol. Once, Henry succeeded in getting a banana into the basket in the middle. And he was allowed to choose any prize he wanted. He chose a huge fluffy tiger. Henry walked with pride through the fairgrounds with his prize. The tiger is still in their apartment's living room.

The family's favourite game was the Camel Race. It always stood at the corner of Spoorlaan and NS Plein. Henry was a fanatic of the Camel Race. They spent some tens of euros every year on the Camel Race but never won more than a small fluffy toy. Once, Henry deliberately went during the Children's Afternoon, thinking he had better chances then; but then he always ended up last in the race. That was funny.

At the intersection of the Spoorlaan and the Heuvelring was the Super Swing 'Around the World'. (It had chairs attached by a chain to a revolving wheel, which gradually rose as it whirled faster.) This ride had won the 'public prize' a number of times. Carol heard her youngest daughter saying, "Mama, do not be such a sissy. This ride goes really slow." She glanced at Henry who nodded with a smile.

"Okay, then." said Carol hesitantly.

"Papa, buy tickets right away, before Mama changes her mind," called the youngest daughter. And thus, she allowed herself to take the ride.

When the wheel started to rise, she really found it scary. Henry wanted to hold her hand to assure her, but she had grabbed her chair so tightly and did not want to release it. Henry saw that she had also shut her eyes. "Look, Carol. It really is a beautiful view. You can see the roof of the ABN-AMRO building." he said. Carol tried opening one eye; that was less scary. And she slowly got used to the height, eventually opening both eyes. But the wheel had already started to descend... Henry and her daughter laughed at her after the ride. "I am quite proud of myself!" she said in her defence, laughing.

And there, stood Carol, in front of the Super Swing. She parked her walker next to the ticket counter and bought a ticket. "For you, ma'am?" asked the surprised woman selling the tickets.

"Sure," smiled Carol. "What does she think of me. A ninety-year-old woman who is looking for a little excitement?" thought Carol. As the Super Swing rose, Carol's eyes were open. She wanted to see the view that Henry wanted her to see. She felt the wind kiss her cheeks like they did before. "Tilburg is indeed beautiful." But Carol knew that already.

Carol and Henry came to the Netherlands when they were twenty-five years old; and they came to Tilburg. They were called 'migrants' then; and in the 1990s (and long after) they were called *allochtoon*. Now, everybody is simply 'Tilburger'. Carol wanted to return to her home country when her youngest daughter reached eighteen years old. But both daughters protested when they heard her plan. "So, you want our future children to grow up without a grandfather and grandmother, just like us," they said. So much for that plan. Carol decided then to love Tilburg. And she never regretted it. Tilburg is a wonderful city to love.

And then, the Super Swing started to descend. Carol took a good look at the city, and closed her eyes... never to open them again...

Maya Butalid, August 2007

Note: This was originally written in Dutch, as a final assignment of a story writing workshop that I attended. It got a '*stimuleringsprijs*'.

Chapter 18
Living with Corona

The pandemic brought with it valuable insights and possibilities for a new normal.

It was Thursday evening on March 12, 2020, when Carlo and I were anxiously watching the first Corona press conference of the Dutch government on TV. It was clear that the country was dealing with a crisis, an unprecedented crisis, a crisis with so many unknowns. During this press conference Prime Minister Rutte announced a number of far-reaching directives. Schools were to be closed starting on Monday, March 16. Restaurants, cafes, sports and fitness clubs, saunas and sex clubs were to be closed starting the following Sunday evening of March 15. People were asked to work as much as possible from home. The government made a list of vital work and professions, those who were exempted from this call, such as health workers, caregivers in the homes for the aged, police, supermarket employees and those who worked in the distribution of vital goods and services. Travel with public transportation, like trains and buses, should only be done for very necessary trips. In accordance with these directives, business establishments and most offices were immediately closed. A few days later, on March 19, all homes for the aged were closed to all visitors.

The first official Corona case was on February 27, in Tilburg (the city where we live). It was actually somebody from the neighbouring town of Loon op Zand, but the person was hospitalized in Tilburg. Soon enough Tilburg and the province of North Brabant became the hot spot of Corona cases. It felt weird and a bit scary to be living in the hot spot of Corona. North Brabant was not put in isolation from the rest of the country, people could still travel to and from North Brabant. So, Carlo and I still continued to go to Amersfoort and Utrecht to babysit our grandchildren. But after two weeks, just before the first Corona press conference on March 12, we decided to suspend our babysitting, as we started to get worried about getting the virus. Especially with Carlo's underlying health condition, he actually belongs in the high-risk category. Getting sick with Corona could be severe for him.

Torn between fear and responsibility
While most offices were closed, our office (*Vluchtelingenwerk*/Council for Refugees in Tilburg) remained open. *Vluchtelingenwerk* was not in the list of vital and crucial establishments which were supposed to remain open, but we decided to remain open anyway. We found it important to continue to be accessible to our clients, the newcomer refugees. This is the group of refugees whose applications for asylum had very recently been approved. They still have very little knowledge about the Dutch system and society, and do not yet speak and understand the Dutch language. Stopping our assistance to them could lead to financial problems such as delays in the processing of their social security benefits, delays in the payments of their house rents, electricity, etc. We of course made some adjustments in our work protocols, such as assisting them only by appointment. In my case I decided to only go to our office if a physical consultation with a refugee client was really

necessary and could not be done via WhatsApp messaging or video calling.

The overwhelming feeling, I had, in the first two months was fear, combined with a continuous inner struggle with the issue of responsibility. On the one hand I felt responsible towards our refugee clients who needed our help, so I could not refrain from going to our office. On the other hand, I felt a responsibility towards Carlo. Exposing myself to the virus is not only taking a risk for my own health but also that of Carlo's. And in a way, I also felt responsible towards my daughters, since Carlo is of course their father, and they do not want their father (and me) to get sick. And on a broader perspective I felt responsible towards the whole community; that I should do as much as I can to help stop the spreading of the virus. Dilemmas which kept on playing in my mind. It was quite exhausting actually.

After two months, my fear subsided; and 'just being careful' took its place.

Valuable insights and possibilities

Then I started to see the advantages and possibilities brought about by the pandemic. On a personal level, I started biking again, as it was safer to go to work by bike than with the bus. I stopped using my bike several years ago, after I had a terrible fall. Since then, I had been coming up with excuses, why it is better not to go by bike. With the pandemic, the reason to pick up that bike again was quite convincing. Aside from the fact that it was safer to go by bike in the midst of the pandemic, it was also healthy, good for the environment and for my savings. Talking about savings, we were also able to cut down on a lot of expenses—like on public transportation as we refrained from travelling outside Tilburg and dining out. Our planned vacations were cancelled.

On a broader societal level, the pandemic also brought valuable insights and possibilities for a better 'new normal'. The closing of the schools, for example, forced parents to combine work (working from home) with assisting their children in their home and online lessons. Combining work and the care for the children have always been what most mothers do. But for the first time, many fathers were also able to experience this first hand during the pandemic. This is a good thing. By experiencing this first hand, many fathers (I hope) will learn to value how it is to combine work and the care for the children. Hopefully, this will lead to more fathers participating more in the care for children after the pandemic is over.

The pandemic also brought with it a different perspective about working from home. Having experienced this, more and more companies have become more open to this arrangement. Many companies are planning to have their workers work from home part of their time, even after the pandemic is over. Working from home actually has a lot of advantages. It is more economical for some companies as they need less office space. It is good for the environment, as it reduces the use of cars. It will help solve the problem of traffic and overloaded trains during rush hours. And an important advantage, in my opinion, is that it will give women (and men) more flexibility in combining work and the care for their children and household.

The pandemic also made visible and felt the importance of health workers, teachers, those working in the supermarkets and in the distribution of vital goods and services. Health workers are now even seen as the new heroes of society. I just hope that this appreciation will be expressed in better compensation for their work. (The Dutch government gave a one-time thousand-euro bonus to all hospital workers—from nurses to cleaners, but except doctors. But the government has so far refused to raise their salaries.)

The pandemic, however, also made more visible the 'cracks' in our society. With the closing of the schools, children already in a disadvantaged position (due to poverty, or for having parents who are less involved in the education of their children for whatever reason) were put in a more disadvantaged position by having to miss lessons. Investing on more parent—involvement in the education of their children should be continuously addressed. Programs in this direction should be made an integral part of the education system. Another issue which came to light is the plight of children and women suffering from domestic violence. With the closing of the schools, these children lost their most important safe haven, their school.

Parents working from home for a long period of time, combined with having to care for their children and household, resulted in a lot of stress and tension within many households; this became a fertile ground for domestic violence. Addressing the problem of domestic violence has never been so validated as in this time of the pandemic.

A crisis gets the best out of people.
There is this saying that 'a crisis gets the best or the worst out of people'. I choose to believe in the first, that a crisis gets the best out of people. This is also what I saw in the height of the Corona crisis. Lots of spontaneous initiatives of people or groups of people started to prop up. One particular initiative which warmed my heart was the so-called 'bear hunting'. People all over The Netherlands started putting teddy bears in their windows for children to find when they go 'bear hunting' in the

neighbourhood. Since all day-cares and schools were closed, and all recreation establishments for children were also closed, this 'bear hunting' activity provided a nice alternative for the children. I even experienced this when our three-year-old grandson stayed with us for a couple of days. We took a walk in the neighbourhood, and he noticed all those bears in the windows of several houses. And he started to look for bears, so excitedly, as we walked around the neighbourhood. Such pure and simple fun!

Another initiative worth mentioning is the WeCare.NL. This was started by somebody I know in Tilburg, and this initiative rolled out to other cities. Through this initiative people could make a donation, the money raised was then used to buy restaurant gift cards which were given to health workers as a gesture of appreciation for being frontline workers in the fight against Corona. At the same time, this also gave support to restaurant owners who were affected very badly by the crisis because of the closing down of their restaurants for months. Hitting two birds with one stone, genius!

Another initiative which popped up in Tilburg was ONS Soepje. This group of volunteers distributed daily free freshly prepared soup and meals to about 250 households affected by the crisis. Then there were individual initiatives of people, one of whom is an ex-colleague, who offered the elderly to do their groceries for them. Since the elderly people belong to the high-risk group, many of them were afraid to go out of the house to do their groceries during the height of the crisis.

There were so many more spontaneous initiatives from people all over the country that I could not name them all here. But my point is, in times of crisis people tend to help and reach out to each other.

The importance of good governance
I am thankful and I feel very fortunate to be in a country where there is good governance in this time of the pandemic. The Dutch government is actually handling the pandemic crisis quite well. The weekly Corona press conferences of the government, at the onset of the crisis, were an important source of support for me. The guidelines laid out by the government were clear and well substantiated. I could see that the government policies were backed up by medical and scientific experts. It was clear that the priority task at hand for the government was to secure the health of the people. The economic impact of the pandemic was tremendous. But at the height of the virus outbreak, the message of the government was clear—that the health of the people is crucial in getting out of the economic crisis. This, however, was put under tremendous pressure when the pandemic continued to rage. By mid-April 2021, the Netherlands was already in the middle of the third wave of the Corona pandemic. Health considerations were not just about not getting sick with Corona but were also about the psychological impact the pandemic had on the people. Also, the economic impact the pandemic had on the people continued to grow and was becoming intolerable.

The parliament also held regular debates on the issue of Corona. Except for two far-right political parties, all other political parties never politicized the Corona crisis. The debates focused on how best to handle the pandemic and its social and economic impact, with the welfare of all groups of people in mind. The problem pertaining to children in disadvantaged positions and domestic violence were, for example, discussed in parliament. How to best help freelancers and small entrepreneurs greatly affected by the pandemic was also a point of discussion in parliament.

How the various political parties handled themselves during the height of the outbreak gave me a feeling of confidence and trust. I have witnessed how mature our democracy is here in The Netherlands. That is a comforting thought.

Another aspect of good governance is the country's social infrastructure: such as having universal health care, universal and compulsory education and the system of unemployment benefits. These are very well established in The Netherlands. This pandemic has shown us that universal health care is really indispensable. Obligatory education ensured that all schools organized and set up very quickly the home/online education for all schoolchildren when the schools were closed down. The system of unemployment benefits served as an essential safety net for the many people who lost their jobs due to the pandemic. If these social infrastructures were not in place, the health, social and economic impact of the pandemic would have been far greater.

Intelligent lockdown
While the guidelines made by the government were far-reaching, there was really no complete lockdown imposed in The Netherlands. People were asked to stay at home as much as possible during the height of the Corona outbreak, but it was never prohibited to go out. The government put more emphasis on social distancing. Many times, Prime Minister Rutte would tell the people in his press conferences to keep at least a 1.5-metre distance from each other when jogging or walking, for example, in the park. He would even add that outdoor exercise is important for our health, so people should continue to do this, but to do it with social distancing.

Rutte described our type of lockdown in The Netherlands as an 'intelligent lockdown'. This means that people could weigh the considerations for themselves to what extent they stay at home. But one thing is clear, if one goes out of the house, they should always observe social distancing. This kind of lockdown puts more emphasis on the personal responsibility of the people. People are made to actively think for themselves how best to avoid getting the virus. This is quite a responsibility.

In June 2020, the guidelines had already been eased. The elementary and high schools were already fully opened, after a transition period of being fifty percent open. The schools for tertiary education (colleges and universities) are still preparing though to open up after the summer holidays in September. Restaurants, cafes, sports and fitness clubs, museums, movie houses and cultural centres, and the so-called 'contact professions' such as hairdressers, physical therapists, manicurists and pedicurists have been allowed to operate. Churches have also resumed their services. And travelling by public transportation is no longer limited to very essential travel. Except for the elementary and high schools, the guideline of maintaining 1.5-metre distance still has to be observed. The wearing of face masks is only required in public transportation, where the 1.5-metre distancing cannot be guaranteed. The last Corona press conference of the government after the first wave was on June 24, wherein the plan for the loosening up of the guidelines was laid out. This marked the end of the crisis period, so we thought. In that press conference Rutte reiterated the importance of maintaining social distancing, for we may have gotten out of the crisis, but the Corona virus is still with us. And indeed, the virus was still with us. Even before the summer was over there were already signs that the pandemic was entering into its second wave. The cabinet had to cut short its summer break to address the looming second wave of the Corona virus.

With the easing down of the guidelines, people also started to loosen up. Some places like shopping areas and markets began to be crowded with people. This led to the public debate whether or not to make the wearing of face masks mandatory in public places, especially those places wherein the 1.5 metre distancing is not being observed. In response to this public debate, the government announced that it will not make this mandatory on the national level, but that the mayors may have the prerogative to impose this in their respective city or town. And in response to this, the mayors of Amsterdam and Rotterdam immediately announced that they will make the wearing of face masks mandatory in selected public areas which tended to be crowded with people starting August 5. This again led to a lot of public discussion and debate whether such an order is legally possible. Wearing face masks is seen as a form of curtailment of one's freedom, and the government can only impose restrictions of one's freedom in times of crisis. But we were already out of the crisis!

With more than a year of the pandemic, we already had a taste of stricter Corona guidelines such as the curfew, being allowed to receive only one visitor per day and wearing of face mask in all public indoor places. People are already Corona-tired, but nevertheless most people still follow the Corona guidelines. I already tested twice, but fortunately both with negative results. Both Carlo and I already got our first vaccination in March 2021, and the second shot is scheduled in May. Nonetheless, we will continue to follow the Corona guidelines for as long as we deem them necessary, until the Corona no longer poses a threat to public health. This is to me a matter of personal responsibility.

It's been more than a year that I have not hugged my

daughters Ligaya and Elena. It's been more than a year that I have not kissed the cheeks of friends when seeing them. It's been more than a year that I have not shaken hands with people when meeting them. I guess this is what I miss the most, human personal touch, such a basic ingredient in connecting with people. Only time will tell when this will again be possible.

Part 3
Identity

When people ask me where I am from, I would often (half mischievously) answer "Tilburg" (the city I live in). After having spent more than half of my life in the Netherlands, it would be rather simplistic for me to answer, "the Philippines", though. I belong to two places: the Philippines and the Netherlands. Both places have shaped my identity. While I am truly 'at home' in the Philippines, I have 'adapted to living' in the Netherlands; but these concepts are difficult to define in practice.

Take language: Carlo and I speak Cebuano at home; I speak Dutch/Cebuano with my children; speak Tagalog/Cebuano with other Filipinos; speak Dutch with my colleagues; read in Dutch and English; watch TV programs in English, Dutch, or other languages (with Dutch subtitles).

Language is an important aspect of identity; and it is obvious that my languages and identity are a bit mixed.

My children have it simpler. They were born and raised in the Netherlands, and it is easy for them to answer "Tilburg" when asked where they are from. For them, the Philippines is the place their parents are from; they are Dutch of Philippine descent.

Since we arrived in the Netherlands, we have been able to choose between two templates (the Philippines' and the Netherlands') of how to do things. I like to think that I have chosen the best from both; but a lot may be a strange mix of both, or mere chance. And there are a lot of things that are just 'me'—

that do not really come from either culture.

One's identity is not static, but dynamic. As you go through life you are constantly creating and recreating your identity. And as you go through this process, you do not lose yourself, but rather enrich yourself. Having said this, I know that an important part of me will always be Filipino, me being a Filipino immigrant.

Chapter 19
Mama, am I Filipino or Dutch?

'Raising children in a mixed culture is a process of constant dialogue and interaction.'

I'm a mother of two children. I am married to a Filipino. Carlo and I came to the Netherlands in 1983. Our daughters were born here: Ligaya and Elena. In this article I will share mostly some conversations I had with Ligaya when she was still a child. As my eldest daughter I had to deal with her the most on how it is to bring up a child in a mixed culture. When she was growing up as a child, I was still grappling with how to deal with the Dutch culture. When Elena grew up (she is five years younger than Ligaya) I was already more relaxed with the Dutch culture, having found a good mix between my Filipino roots and the Dutch culture.

Carlo and I are both Cebuanos, we talk in Cebuano at home. Our family was in the Philippines when Ligaya was just learning to speak, and so her first language is also Cebuano.

However, when we went back to the Netherlands, Ligaya had difficulties expressing herself with other Dutch children in the *creche* (nursery). This worried us, and for a while we considered the idea of talking in Dutch with her at home. Fortunately, the *creche leidsters* (caretakers) and other Dutch parents encouraged us to speak our own language at home. They assured us that, soon enough, our daughter will pick up the Dutch language. And true enough, she did! So, at home Ligaya spoke Cebuano, and Dutch in the *creche*. I thought that raising children in a mixed culture was only a question of language... until one day.

Early Years

We were on our way to the *creche* when Ligaya (she was only three years old then) asked me, "Mama, am I Filipino or Dutch?"

For a while I did not know what to say. I first had to search my own feelings. With uncertainty, I answered her, "Well, you are, of course, a Filipino because we, your parents, are Filipinos, and we try to live as Filipinos. But an important part of you is also Dutch because you were born here, live here and most of your friends are Dutch."

Ligaya responded happily, "Oh, how nice! I am 'two'!" (i.e., Filipino and Dutch) "You and Papa are only 'one', right? And Ember (her Dutch friend) is also only 'one'. But I am 'two'!"

And with more certainty I answered her back, "Yes, and you are lucky to be 'two'."

This conversation with Ligaya made me realize that living in a mixed culture need not be problematic—or rather, it can be very enriching to one's life. Also, I learned that as parents trying to raise our children in two cultures, it is important to find out how our children perceive and experience their life in these two cultures.

Of course, the lessons I learned are easier said than done. One day, when Ligaya was four years old (she was then at the *kleuterklas* or kindergarten), she asked me, "Mama, could we not just talk in Dutch, so I do not need to think always in Cebuano and then in Dutch?"

"Okay, do not learn Cebuano anymore. And when I go back

to the Philippines, you may not come with me, and you will stay at home alone!"

Surprised, Ligaya calmly asked me, "Mama, why are you angry?" Indeed, why was I angry? I thought.

I said, "I'm sorry I got angry. I was just hurt because it is important for me that you know my language. This is the language of your family, your roots. And I just want you to be able to communicate with the rest of your family back home. Of course, I understand that you will prefer to speak more in Dutch. But please do not forget our language."

Then she said, "Okay."

That evening I kept thinking about that conversation. While a part of me was telling me not to impose my own thinking and feelings on her; I also wanted to ensure the Filipino identity of my daughter. Carlo and I thought that perhaps we should make a compromise. The following day we told Ligaya that she may talk to us in Dutch while we continue to speak to her in Cebuano. She was pleased with the arrangement.

At the age between five and six years, Ligaya continued to grapple with her own identity. There was a time when she wished her hair was blond, or that she had a lighter skin colour, or that she was a little taller, etc. Patiently, we dealt with every question but there were times when I also lost my temper, especially if she complained about food. Fortunately, Ligaya also received positive remarks from her social environment such as how nice her hair was because it is black and thick; how lucky she was to have such a skin colour the whole year round without having to sunbathe, etc.

In the case of my youngest daughter Elena, she did not seem to be grappling too much with her identity. When she was still of elementary school age, she once told us that she is actually a

Dutch imprisoned in a Filipino body. And all I could do was just laugh about it.

Ligaya at Seven

When Ligaya was seven years old, I felt she was beginning to get hold of her own identity. When somebody told her that she is small, she would answer with confidence, "Yes, I'm small here, but in the Philippines I'm just average." She also seemed to have accepted the fact that I will always be her *kleine moeder* (small mother). Once, I overheard her teaching her classmate some Cebuano words. And when her classmate stayed with us for the weekend, she was so happy because her classmate especially enjoyed our meals. Proudly she told her: "That's Filipino food. That's what we always eat for dinner."

Raising children in a mixed culture is a long process. From my experience, it was a process of constant dialogue and interaction with my daughter—trying to find out and understand her own thinking and feelings while also making her aware of my own. As parents we cannot impose ourselves upon our children. We can only interact with them, explain to them as much as we can, and build a relationship of mutual respect. We should give our children space to discover their own identity. We cannot define that identity for them, but we can only guide them and try to give answers. Children are capable of understanding things better than we think they can.

Travelling

In the summer of 1991, I took Ligaya and Elena to Sweden for a meeting. Since we had Philippine passports, we needed to get visas for Sweden and transit visas for Germany and Denmark (since we were travelling by train). While we were packing our things, Ligaya asked why we needed to have a stamp in our passports.

I answered her, "Well, these are called visas. Each country makes its own rules and one of these rules says that visitors should ask permission to enter a particular country. So, that's what we need visas for. "

Then she said: "So, if my classmates go to Sweden, they will also have to get visas."

And I automatically answered, "No, they do not have to."

"Why?" she asked.

I started to get nervous, anticipating where the conversation was leading to. "Well, because your classmates have Dutch passports, and those with Dutch passports do not need to get visas for Sweden."

"Why?"

And I answered, "Well, as I had told you, each country makes its own rules and that's one of those rules."

"Oh", she said, "can we not just get Dutch passports? After all, we're living in the Netherlands, just like my classmates."

At that point, I felt something I could not really describe. It was a mixture of many feelings: pain, anger, sadness, uncertainty, homesickness... Calmly, I told her. "Oh, my child, you ask so many questions. Sometimes you'll have to wait until you're a bit older. And you'll understand these things better." And quickly I asked her. "Have you packed all the toys and things you want to take along?"

And she answered, "Yes."

In 1994 we decided to acquire Dutch citizenship. While Carlo and I still feel and consider ourselves as Filipinos, we have also realized that as overseas Filipinos residing in the Netherlands for more than ten years, we have also become part of the Dutch society. We felt the need to participate actively and establish our roles and our place both in the Philippine and Dutch societies.

We wanted to acquire Dutch citizenship for our children too. This would enable us to better support and guide them in securing their rights and place as members of the society where they live, while helping them maintain their Filipino identity.

Entering Puberty

This period brought with it another dimension of parenting. At this age, establishing one's identity becomes even more important. Being conscious of one's identity goes deeper than just knowing 'Who you are' or 'Where you come from?' Our children are also concerned with questions like 'What do I want?' and 'What is important to me? As parents we also begin to realize that our children are on their way to becoming young adults. We start to be more conscious of these questions like 'What kind of adults will they become? What kind of adults do we want them to be?' And these questions influence the way we view their behaviour and our expectations of them. Thus, developing one's values becomes an important dimension in our children's identity.

Values are shaped by our experiences and expectations from our environment. Children in a mixed culture are often confronted with differing and sometimes conflicting experiences and expectations from their environment. Such a situation makes the process of developing one's values extra difficult for our children. And I think, as parents, we should bear this in mind in our efforts at guiding and supporting our children in the formation of their own values.

Pakikiramdam

As Filipino parents, for example, it is only understandable that we want to instil Filipino values in our children while at the same time our children also learn the values of the Western culture. One such Filipino value which I found important for my children to acquire is *pakikiramdam* (feeling for another). *Pakikiramdam* refers to the heightened awareness and sensitivity for the other by paying attention to subtle cues and non-verbal behaviour. When Ligaya was about eleven or twelve years old, there were times when I would scold her when she came to me for favours while I was pre-occupied.

"Can't you see that I'm already having a hectic time?" Is what I would tell her.

To which she would react, "Why are you so upset? You do not have to say 'Yes' anyway. You can just say 'No', you know. Is that too much of a problem for you?"

And I would explain to her (sometimes impatiently), "You see, you should realize that, as your mother, I always try to meet all your needs. My children are high in my priorities. So, when you come to me with requests, you should assume that I always take them seriously. So, on your part, I also expect you to have already processed your requests. That is, ask yourself if it's the right time to come to me with those requests, are they that urgent for me to drop the other things I'm doing to attend to your requests, or can you do them yourself, so your mother won't be stressed. That's consideration."

Such a conversation happened many times, and it was quite obvious that she did not really get the point. After all, they were taught at school to be assertive by (verbally) expressing their needs and opinions. And that you, yourself as a person, are responsible for your own well-being.

It was only when we went to the Philippines when Ligaya understood and felt what *pakikiramdam* was all about. She was so surprised when my father packed all the mangoes he had and gave them to her after we had dinner at his house. She asked me later, "How did *Lolo* guess that I like mangoes?" Also, she felt very guilty when my sister offered her own bed with a mattress after she overheard her asking me, "Are we sleeping here in this bed without a mattress?"

So, I told her, "That's why you just do not say things without processing them first. Always think what it can mean for the other person."

There were numerous other incidents when Ligaya experienced what *pakikiramdam* was all about. On the plane, on our way back to the Netherlands, she told me, "I guess I now understand what you always tell me about processing first my requests." It was then that I realized how important our Philippine trips were for our children. It was the only way for them to experience, understand and feel the Filipino culture, so that they may integrate elements of this in their own identity and set of values.

Relationships

Another important concern of Filipino mothers is the relationships of their teenage daughters. The difference in values between the Filipino and the Dutch culture on this matter is enormous. This difference is further accentuated by the generation gap. For example, Filipino girls (at least, in my time and social circles) were taught to wait for the boys to court them or were discreet in showing their feelings towards the opposite sex. It is not proper for girls to run after the boys. In fact, girls were encouraged to play 'hard-to-get'. When I told my daughters about this, they found it amusing.

Our daughters live in a culture and generation where it is no big deal for a girl to ask a boy to be her steady boyfriend. This does not really bother me. After all, I was not the type who played 'hard-to-get' anyway. Carlo had to ask me only once, and I immediately said, "Yes."

A more serious matter for me, however, is pre-marital sex and 'live-in' relationships. Pre-marital sex is normal in Dutch society. Dutch youths do not talk about whether or not they should have pre-marital sex, but rather at which age they should have it. Once, we were watching a talk show on TV about young pregnancies. Reacting to a sixteen-year-old mother, Ligaya commented. "Well, I find sixteen too young to have sex with your boyfriend."

To which I responded, "What age are you then planning to have sex with your boyfriend?" (This was only a theoretical question as she had no boyfriend at that point.)

To which she nonchalantly answered, "Eighteen, maybe?"

I frowned at her. She asked, "Why? At what age then?" And I said, "The longer you wait, the better."

'Live-in' (*samenwonen*) relationships are accepted and even officially recognized by the Dutch government as a legitimate type of serious long-term relationship, just like marriage. Once, I overheard my two daughters' conversation. Both of them said that they will probably first have a live-in relationship before getting married.

Then Elena said, "Well, I think I'll marry first before I start to have children of my own."

Having lived in the Netherlands for some decades, I have already learned to view (sexual) relationships from various perspectives. Within the context of the Dutch society, I have seen that pre-marital sex could very well be a part of the normal, healthy process of establishing a relationship with one's partner. And a 'live-in' relationship, like marriage, is just another form of serious long-term relationship with one's partner.

Independence

Independence is also one thing which children in the Netherlands are taught in school. At a young age they already learn to form their own opinion. Gathering the right information, processing them and coming up with their own conclusions is part of the training they get as early as in the elementary school. So, both Ligaya and Elena grew up to be independently-minded. As a Filipino parent it actually took me some time to get used to this. When Elena was studying in the university, she told me one day that she decided to be an officer of their students' rowing association. She said that this was actually a full-time undertaking, meaning that she will be delayed for a year with her studies. And I responded, "I will have to think it over if I will allow you to do that."

To which she responded "Ma'am, I am not asking your permission. This is an announcement."

The realization that both my daughters are Dutch

When my daughters were still young and I would be upset with them for their behaviour I would always say, "You are like the Dutch". Like, "Stop having a big mouth, you are like the Dutch" or "You only think of yourself, you are like the Dutch". One time when they were a bit older, I guess they were in high school then, they told us (Carlo and I) to stop always saying that they are like the Dutch. "When you tell us 'we are like the Dutch' when you are upset about something we do, you are actually saying that being Dutch is bad. Don't you realize that we are really Dutch? So, you are actually saying that we are bad." Since then, we stopped saying 'you are like the Dutch' when we were upset with them.

Looking back, I guess we have been quite successful in getting a good mix and balance between the Filipino and Dutch cultures in the upbringing of our children. But in the end, this is something our children will have to conclude themselves.

Chapter 20
Being Allochtoon

From being an allochtoon, to just being me.

In the Netherlands there is this strange concept of an *allochtoon*. People coming from non-Western countries and who reside in the Netherlands, or those who have at least one parent who was born in a non-Western country is considered to be *allochtoon* (plural: *allochtonen*). Strictly speaking *allochtoon* refers to those with a migrant background, but in daily usage it usually refers to people coming from non-Western countries or whose parents were born in non-Western countries. Since Carlo and I were born in the Philippines, we and our children are considered to be *allochtoon*.

Many native Dutch associate those considered *allochtonen* as not being fully integrated in Dutch society, having difficulties with the Dutch language, and having a lower educational level. Many government policies and programs directed at the *allochtonen* usually addresses these problems. Elementary and high schools with *allochtoon* children get, for example, an additional subsidy from the government to be used for extra tutorials for their *allochtoon* school children.

Being an *allochtoon* had always been a part of my consciousness. Or I would rather say, when you are an *allochtoon* in the Netherlands you would almost always be confronted with the fact of your being *allochtoon*. When I was new in my job as a coordinator of a parenting program my boss had told one Dutch para-professional under my supervision that she should support me because I am a Filipina (read: an *allochtoon*). I am not really hierarchical in my style of supervision; I give people whom I supervise a lot of room to do things that they deem necessary for their work. I also involve them as much as possible in our work processes. My boss felt that I was giving this Dutch para-professional too much freedom, so he stepped in and controlled her actions. This Dutch para-professional did not like this and told him, in my presence, that it was his idea that she should support me because I was a Filipina. That was when I learned of my boss's 'instructions'. Although I did not make a fuss about it, my boss profusely explained to me that the para-professional must have misunderstood him.

Although my boss' initial lack of confidence in my capability was exacerbated by the fact that I was not white, I told him that this was his management prerogative. Anyway, at that time, he still did not know what I was capable of doing. But it did occur to me that as an *allochtoon* you first need to prove yourself.

Another incident when I was reminded of my being an *allochtoon* was when I got the position as *individueel trajectbegeleider* (career counsellor) in the institution where I worked. I had this consultation with a Dutch colleague. What I did not know was that she also vied for the position that was just granted to me. During our meeting she told me that she actually also vied for my position and that she was disappointed because it was given to 'just anybody', while she has an **HBO** (*hoger beroepsonderwijs*, higher professional level) diploma. She sort of implied to me, that I was given preferential treatment because I was an *allochtoon*. I felt insulted but ignored the remark and went on with our meeting. Later, she could not resist and asked me directly what my educational background was. I replied curtly, "I studied Psychology at the Tilburg University". This Dutch colleague was obviously taken aback—my educational level was higher than hers. Although I knew that I had put her in her place, I went home that day feeling bad because I was uncomfortable with having to wave my credentials. I bet if I were white, it would not have occurred to her that my credentials were maybe less than hers.

I remember one discussion that I had in my class in cross-cultural psychology in which we discussed how to help *allochtoon* students and children of migrants succeed better in school. One of the Dutch students suggested that the standard for *allochtoon* students should be adjusted such that it will be easier for them to get their diploma. I reacted strongly against the suggestion. "If you have a different set of standards for *allochtoon* students, then that would also make their diploma have a lower value than the 'regular' diplomas. If we are really sincere about helping *allochtoon* students to cope, we should provide more support services to them instead of lowering the standards by which they are assessed."

When I started to work in a Dutch institution, I was aware of the fact that I did not speak nor write perfect Dutch. I would then ask the secretary of our department to correct my grammar before sending out any of my letters. Our secretary found my request quite peculiar. Seemingly I was the only *allochtoon* in our office who wanted my Dutch language corrected. Other *allochtoon* colleagues would feel offended if their Dutch language would be corrected. I told her that I did not want to spend hours trying to write a letter in good Dutch when I could do something more productive. I used this arrangement as an opportunity to improve my mastery of the Dutch language. I would then compare the reworked version of my letter with the original version that I wrote to learn from the corrections that had been made. Eventually our secretary told me that I no longer needed to give my letters to her for corrections as my written Dutch was already good enough.

Being seen as an *allochtoon*, I felt that there were certain expectations people had of me. When I told, for example, my boss about Ligaya's choice of high school, he was quite surprised why she was going to a high school with predominantly white students. He, for example, sent his child to an elementary school with many children of migrants, because he wanted his child to be exposed to the multicultural Dutch society. I told my boss that "being an *allochtoon*, my considerations are different from yours. We are already confronted daily with the fact that we have a different cultural background. So, we do not need to be exposed to the Dutch multicultural society, since we are right in the middle of it." Besides, Carlo and I value academic excellence, something we brought with us from our upbringing in the Philippines. Both Ligaya and Elena qualified for the *HAVO-VWO* high school. This is the type of high school which prepares students for higher professional and academic education. And the *HAVO-VWO* high school they chose was known for its excellent academic training and happened to have predominantly white students.

As an *allochtoon* I also felt that I needed to be 'loyal' to my *allochtoon* group. In one meeting of those involved in the **Opstap** program (a parenting program which targeted poor families with children aged four to six years old), when the topic revolved around the problems of migrant families, I brought up the problem of Dutch families. We had always been discussing about the problems of migrant families. But Dutch families also have problems. In fact, I have the impression that their problems are more complicated. With the migrant families, the problems seem to be mainly related to them having a different cultural background, problems in understanding the Dutch systems and a lack of mastery of the Dutch language. But with the Dutch families living on social security subsidies, the problems I encountered in families participating in the *Opstap* program were far more complex, like drug addiction, excessive alcohol use, excessive gambling, living in debt, social isolation, distressed single parents, children caught in the tug-of-war between divorcing parents, and even child abuse. These cannot be addressed by the regular *Opstap* program alone. So, in that meeting I made an appeal that we should develop some kind of an '*Opstap Plus*' program for the Dutch families. This was approved and I was tasked to start an experimental group of Dutch families for the *Opstap Plus* program. I was of course happy that my point was taken, but I was also disturbed why I had to be the one to bring up the issue of the poor Dutch families. Two other coordinators of the program were Dutch. It felt like I was 'betraying' the *allochtoon* families. In the first place, that program was especially designed for the *allochtoon* families, and here I was, an *allochtoon* myself wanting to use extra resources of the program for the Dutch families.

Another instance when I felt I was not loyal to my *allochtoon* group was when I participated in the quality management team of the institution where I worked. Our team was tasked to evaluate our institution and come up with proposals how to obtain a quality certification. When we presented our evaluation and proposals to the rest of our colleagues, I was taken aback by the intense reactions of our Turkish colleagues. We forgot to evaluate the institution in terms of multiculturality! I forgot to inject the issue of the migrant! I almost cried. I felt it was my fault, and I felt like a traitor to my kind when I did not represent the migrants' issues.

From being an *allochtoon* to just being me

All this grappling with being an *allochtoon* actually occurred in my first twenty to twenty-five years in the Netherlands. I am now in my thirty-eighth year living in the Netherlands. There was a point in time, I could not remember anymore exactly when, when I realized that people around me (not only those close to me like my colleagues but also people I randomly talk to in the street) no longer deal with me as an *allochtoon*. Well, at least, I did not feel anymore that I am always confronted with the fact that I am an *allochtoon*. It's just me, Maya, the person that I am. I guess I must have evolved.

Both Ligaya and Elena experience their being an *allochtoon* differently. This is logical, since both of them were born in the Netherlands. I have the impression that they are not always confronted with the fact that they are *allochtoon*.

When Elena was in high school, for example, some of her friends would sometimes complain about the *allochtonen*, saying all kinds of bad things about them. To which Elena would say, "Hold on a minute; haven't you noticed that I, an *allochtoon*, am here?"

Her friends would respond, "But you are not an *allochtoon*."

Then, Elena would explain that since both of her parents were born in the Philippines, she is—by definition—an *allochtoon*. "*Allochtoon* people come in all kinds, just like the Dutch, and it is wrong to lump us all together and say bad things about us," she would tell her friends.

In one of our family visits to the Philippines, some of Ligaya's Dutch friends also happened to be there. When I talked with her Dutch friends, the two of them told me that they actually just realized then that Ligaya is a Filipina (read: *allochtoon*), now that they see her among many Filipinos. They never really saw her as different from them, as somebody with another cultural background.

While I find it important that my daughters are conscious of their Filipino cultural background, I am actually happy to see that they are spared the prejudices that go with being an *allochtoon*. I am happy to see that they could just be themselves, Ligaya and Elena, the persons that they are. Like me now, after so many years of being an *allochtoon*, that I could just be me, Maya, the person that I am.

Chapter 21
On Relationships and Marriage

It is good when marriage is a choice, not a social requirement.

My view towards relationships and marriage has changed tremendously in the years since I came to the Netherlands in 1983.

In the Philippines, a relationship has to have a perspective of finally going into marriage. When entering a relationship, one has to have the intention of getting married with the person you have a relationship with. Otherwise, you are not really serious with your relationship. Sexual relationship is also very interconnected with the stage of the relationship you are in. In particular, sex is reserved for married couples. Engaging in premarital sex is frowned upon by society. It is a sin!

There is however a gender bias when it comes to sexual relationships. Unmarried women who engage in sex are more frowned upon by society and are seen as 'women without morals'. Men who do likewise are generally tolerated, and such behaviour is seen as 'part of being a man'. Strangely enough many men desire to have sexual intercourse with their girlfriends; but once this is achieved, they no longer consider their girlfriend as 'marrying material'. Many women likewise prefer their partner to already have some kind of 'sexual experience' when they marry him, so that her husband already knows 'how to handle her with care' during their first night in bed. But of course, this sexual experience will not be with her, as she needs to protect her virginity before marriage, otherwise she will no longer be 'marrying material'. As a young girl I actually found this a very skewed, even ridiculous, attitude towards sexual relationships. But since I believed then in the virtue of virginity, I vowed to myself that I will seek a man to marry who was still a virgin.

Families of young women caught having engaged in sex with their boyfriend feel dishonoured and demand that the boyfriend in question marry her. All the more if the young woman is found to be pregnant. Women in this situation are considered by society as 'already damaged', meaning that no man in his right mind will still want to marry her. This is the reason why the family of the young woman would demand that her boyfriend who 'damaged her chastity' should marry her.

When I was in high school, I had a (girl) friend my age in our neighbourhood who got pregnant. Her boyfriend was also my friend. And I was actually already aware of their sexual relationship which my (girl) friend confided with me. While at that young age I considered virginity a virtue, I surprisingly did not have any judgement about their sexual relationship. I just sort of accepted it as a matter of fact. Anyway, she got pregnant and everybody in the neighbourhood heard about it. She only had brothers, her father was no longer in the picture, and therefore only had her mother who had raised them. All her brothers were really furious about it and demanded that her boyfriend marry her. Her boyfriend was actually also willing to marry her. But her mother was against it. So, they did not marry. This incident became the talk of our neighbourhood. Nobody understood why her mother did not want them to get married. When I told my mother about this, she told me that she actually agreed with the mother. When I asked her why, she said "You do not correct a mistake by making another mistake." She thought that both my (girl)friend and her boyfriend (they were just fifteen!) were still very young and were not yet ready to carry the responsibility of parenthood. The attitude of my mother towards this incident surprised me in a positive way.

Unmarried couples who live together are widely considered in the Philippines as couples who are 'living in sin', with more emphasis on the woman who is 'living in sin'. This was the case at least before I moved to the Netherlands thirty-eight years ago in 1983, although I think that this is still the case to this very day. As a young girl who went to a Catholic high school, I sort of just accepted as a matter of fact that living together, without marrying, just does not fit in a healthy and wholesome relationship. To me a wholesome relationship ran like this: courtship (wherein the boy courts the girl), dating (wherein the girl sees to it that she remains a virgin), a short engagement, then marriage. And since there is no divorce in the Philippines, this marriage should last forever, no matter what.

When I came to the Netherlands in 1983, I learned that engaging in sex is part of dating, that living together is part of the process of a relationship and is even considered as an official form of 'civil status', and that relationships do not necessarily lead to marriage. Many couples consciously choose to live together and build a family together but not get married. In the Philippines you only have three possible civil statuses, either you are single, married or widowed. In the Netherlands you have more—single, living together, married, divorced and widowed. The first time I encountered the word 'living together' in official forms in the Netherlands I was quite amused by it. I was more amused when I saw that there were even greeting cards sold in stores especially made for occasions when couples start to live together.

My attitude towards 'living together' started to change only after having been in The Netherlands for ten years, (1983 to 1993), when I had a colleague whom I also had personal interactions with. This colleague had a family, with three children also around the same age as my own two daughters, and a partner who is the father of her children. She and her partner have been living together for years, and they have raised their children together as a family. And I did not see anything wrong with this. In fact, their family was very loving, there was respect, and the children were brought up in a very responsible way. So, how could this 'living together' be sinful?

This change of my attitude towards 'living together' was however still on a theoretical level. It was when my own daughters started to live together with their boyfriends that I started to deal with it on an emotional level. After a time, I was already okay with it emotionally. Then, surprisingly, first Ligaya, then Elena, decided to get married. Honestly, their decision to get married was to me a pleasant surprise.

In a way, marriage in the Philippines is something which is imposed by society and one's social environment. It is an unwritten requirement for a couple in order to live together and build their own family. And once married, Philippine laws make sure that the couple stay married. In the Netherlands, marriage is something the couple consciously choose to enter into, and it is a conscious decision to stay and remain a married couple. Marriage is a commitment that the couple consciously make to each other. So, in a way, the statement 'for better and for worse' during marriage ceremonies has actually more substance in Dutch marriages, because the couple has to exert conscious effort and make a conscious decision to continue to stay together when they find themselves in bad times. In the Netherlands, married couples have an option not to continue to stay together, they are allowed to divorce by Dutch laws.

Often, I hear parents (especially mothers) of the bride during wedding receptions in the Philippines saying that they are also sad about the marriage of their daughter. In a way, they see the marriage of their daughter as a 'loss', because their daughter would now leave her parent's house to join her husband's family. This is further augmented with the fact that her daughter will now take on the family name of her husband. While I understand why many mothers of Filipina brides think and feel this way; I think about this differently. I see the marriage of my daughters as an addition and enrichment to my family. With the marriage of a daughter, you really do not lose her, but instead you have gained a son. How special could that be?

By the way, in the Netherlands the woman has an option not to take on the family name of her husband. And Ligaya did just that. And if ever the woman chooses to take on the family name of her husband, she still needs to fill up her maiden name in official forms and documents. The main name indicated in my passport for example is my maiden name. The family name of Carlo, in smaller letters, is mentioned to indicate that I am the 'wife of…'

Another aspect which is very much intertwined with relationships and marriage is regarding one's career. Many young men and women nowadays do not think immediately of marriage after finishing their professional education. They are then just starting to build their career, where most of their focus is. In the Netherlands where education is universal, the career possibilities for both men and women are quite wide. One's career is often seen as an important defining factor of who you are as a person, of one's identity. In an individualistic Dutch society, defining one's identity takes a central place for young men and women. So, getting married at this stage of one's life when one is still starting to build a career; a career which will eventually define you as a person—is a rather bold and daring thing to do. By getting married at this stage, the young couple has decided to continue to define each of their individual identities in connectedness with each other. The challenge at hand for this young couple then is to continually seek the balance between 'taking space for yourself and for your self-development and giving space to your partner so that he/she may continue to develop himself/herself'.

As I have learned to see it, especially from the examples of my daughters, marriage is not losing yourself as an individual; but it is rather gaining a partner with whom you can both continue to grow and develop to become the persons you really are. Picture this: a garden with lots of different trees, plants and flowers, each having their own different characteristic features, but together they form a beautiful garden. This is how I see marriage and eventually the family that grows out of it.

Chapter 22
It is Usual to be a Mother and have a Full-time Job

Not being a 'mother' mother type does not mean that you are less of a mother.

When I became a mother, I never gave a thought whether I should stop working. For me, it was quite usual for a mother to work. In the Netherlands, motherhood and work seem to be two different worlds. (In the Netherlands, only twenty-five percent of women have full-time jobs after graduation—the lowest in the European Union.) But I believe that you can be both one hundred percent mother and have a full-time job; these roles are to me not contradictory.

My mother had always worked, as a lawyer in government service. My father was also a lawyer, and his work meant spending most of his time away from home. This meant that my mother raised us mostly by herself. When my elder sister was four years old and had to go to kindergarten, my mother arranged it so that my three-year-old brother, and myself (at two years old), could go with our elder sister in kindergarten. If needed, my mother could come quickly, since she worked nearby. When I was a young girl, I would go with my mother to her office during school vacations. I always liked doing this. I got a good idea of what my mother did at work. I would then play make believe as if I was also working. Later, I also tried to do this with my children, but only very occasionally, just to give them an idea of my work. I practiced the exercises of the *Opstap* program with Elena, for example, and also brought her with me during the commencement programs, group outings and cultural activities of the groups I coordinated. When Ligaya was in high school, she also did some volunteer work in the community where I worked, by helping with our children's summer program. Like my mother, I also wanted to give my children a glimpse of what I was doing in my work.

When I was twelve, my mother went to work in Leyte province. Because Leyte was in another island, she would work one week there, and be the other week at home. During the week that she was there, she had asked our neighbours to keep an eye on us when my father was not around. We quickly became independent. At twelve, I managed our finances, and kept the most important keys of the house when my mother was away working in Leyte province. After a while, an uncle, my mother's younger brother, who was studying stayed with us. It was always messy at home. Then, on the day before my mother was scheduled to return, we would clean up. But if she came home earlier than expected, my mother would see the house in a mess, and we got scolded.

I never had the idea that I missed out, that I lacked something. I had a very good relationship with my mother. I corresponded a lot with her, especially when I was sixteen and went to Manila to study. Manila was so far away that I only came home during school breaks.

While in university, I became involved in the underground opposition movement against President Marcos. Carlo was also in the movement. When we got married, we had always divided our tasks equally. I taught him everything about household tasks.

He grew up in a higher-class family, so they always had servants, a chauffeur and a nanny. He did not need to do any household tasks. Now Carlo cooks better than me.

In 1983, the movement deployed us to the Netherlands in order to organize Filipino migrants in Europe and to gather political support for the Philippine struggle. I was then pregnant, and Ligaya was born in 1984, and Elena in 1989. Our new situation in the Netherlands opened to us the opportunity to discover how to take care of our children, and how to divide the work between us. Once, he was in the train with both children and a big bag. A man stared at him for a long while; finally, he asked if Carlo was a widower. Amazing! On other occasions, people would ask him if he was both a father and mother for the children. To which he would answer that he was simply their father, that caring for children is also a task for fathers which he enjoys doing.

Day-care: ridiculous
I was politically active for the Philippine underground movement during the first ten years that I was in the Netherlands. Eventually, I left the movement; studied Psychology and got a job. In the early years—especially during the time when we had our first born, Ligaya—strange situations would crop up. Once, we arranged a transfer in a train station. Carlo came home from a trip, and I needed to leave right away. Ligaya transferred from my arms to his, and I quickly boarded my train. In another case, we both needed to travel, and we could not find anybody to take care of her for the whole time. So, we had to ask several people to take care of Ligaya in turns for the whole duration of our absence. We then made a list of 'do's and don'ts'. Ligaya would then hand this list over during each turn-over from one babysitter

to another, saying with a smile: 'This is the way to take care of me.' But these were extreme examples. After Elena was born, I stopped travelling abroad for work.

Ligaya went to the day-care when she was one year old; Elena started to go to the day-care when she was still a baby. My family in the Philippines found this to be ridiculous. My sister even proposed that we leave our children in the Philippines, where our relatives could bring them up. And I found that, in turn, ridiculous. I chose to have children, thus I want to raise them myself. I do not understand that people in the Philippines 'subcontract' the raising of their children to a young girl (a *yaya*), with no experience or education in childcare. The caretakers in the day-cares in the Netherlands are required to have a diploma in childcare. I find it very important that my children are taken care of by qualified babysitters. For after all, children learn a lot from their babysitters.

I had also arranged to hire a regular babysitter when my children started going to school (to pick them up from school at three thirty p.m. and babysit them till we could pick them up at around five thirty p.m.). In order to find someone to be their regular babysitter, I went to their school, and asked the *overblijfmoeders* (women who watched over the schoolchildren during their lunchbreak) if one of them would want to be their regular babysitter. Finding a babysitter this way assured me that the school had already done a background check on her, since she was already an *overblijfmoeder* of the school. I found a very good babysitter this way. She babysat Ligaya and Elena after school during their elementary school years.

I combine my full-time work with work for the Filipino community and other volunteer activities. I am always very busy. Things like cleaning the house are not done well or often; after all, one needs to prioritize. I guess I have a lot less guilty feelings about this compared to many Dutch parents. For me, it is quite natural; I do not have the feeling that I am neglecting things. Ligaya once told me, "You are very busy, but you are always there at the important moments. You always take me seriously." I could not wish for a better compliment.

Now both Ligaya and Elena have become mothers too— Ligaya about eight years ago when she had her first child, and Elena almost three years ago. When they became mothers, it was for them a natural thing to do to continue working. Both of them never considered stopping work. In a conversation I had with Elena a few months after she gave birth, she told me this "I like being with my baby, but I am not really a 'mother' mother type". By this she meant that while she enjoys being with her baby, she could not imagine herself spending all her time on the baby and not having to work.

When she said this, she was still on maternity leave. "I actually long to go back to work again," she added.

And I told her "Well, not being a 'mother' mother type does not mean that you are less of a mother. Even having a full-time job, you can still be a very good mother. And I actually find you a very good mother."

To which she replied "That's right. You are also not a 'mother' mother type, but I find you a very good mother. You brought me and Ligaya up to become responsible adults, and we are pretty successful and happy with our lives."

Chapter 23
On Women Emancipation

Filipinas are more emancipated than Dutch women.

Once a Dutch person told me that I am so emancipated, and in the same breath added that I must already be very 'Dutchified'. To which I answered readily, "No, I got this from my mother." Many would think that since the Netherlands is a Western developed country, that the emancipation of women here is already complete. And in still developing countries, such as the Philippines, women there still need to emancipate themselves. But on the contrary, the Philippines ranked much higher than the Netherlands in the overall Global Gender Gap Index in 2018 of the World Economic Forum (meaning, that the gender gap in the Philippines is much smaller than that in the Netherlands). The Philippines ranked eighth place, while the Netherlands lagged behind in the twenty-seventh place. This gender gap index measured the following—economic participation and opportunity, educational attainment, health and survival, and political empowerment.

I am actually not surprised to see that the Philippines ranks way higher than the Netherlands in the global gender gap index.

Looking into the past of the Philippines, women had important positions in society before Spain colonized the Philippines more than four hundred years ago. In those times, there were many women priestesses, called the *Babaylanes*.

These *Babaylanes* were the leaders of the local communities. However, when Spain colonized the Philippines, from 1565 to 1898, the women were made subservient. The position of women in society was brought to zero. So, for the record, it was actually the West which made women in the Philippines subservient. But despite this, the strong position of Filipinas in pre-Spanish colonial society seems to have stuck in our collective memory.

I remember, for example, in the late 1970s that the indigenous Kalinga women from the northern part of the Philippines played a very active role in the protests against the building of the Chico River Dam. The dam would have inundated the ancestral lands of the Kalingas. During the height of the protests, the Kalinga women strove to prevent the entry of a truck that was bringing in construction materials. Physical struggle ensued, and in the midst of this the women (mothers and even grandmothers) removed their clothes and lined up to block the road. The trucks withdrew. The news about this somehow made an impression in my young mind.

When Ligaya was still in high school she once told me that she was surprised to learn that the grandmothers of her Dutch classmates only had at most a high school education; while her grandmothers (my mother and Carlo's mother) were both professionals, my mother having finished Law School and Carlo's mother having finished teacher training It was then that I realized that the position of women in the Philippines with respect to educational attainment was better than that of the women in the Netherlands.

Looking at the political empowerment of women, the Philippines has already had two women presidents; while I do not see the Netherlands having a woman prime minister in the years to come.

So no, I am not surprised that the Philippines ranks much better than the Netherlands in the global gender gap index. And my being emancipated is not because I am already 'Dutchified'. I guess I learned to be emancipated from my mother, from her example. And I tend to believe that this also comes from our collective memory as Filipinas, which somehow continues to find its way to manifest itself after having been subdued for years by the Spanish colonizers.

When I think about emancipation, what readily comes to my mind is having a career as a woman. Having a career and having children are often thought of as two things which do not go well together, as something you have to choose. I often hear young women who are still in the midst of building their career saying that 'the moment is not yet right' to start having children. But is there really a 'right moment'? In one of my conversations with Ligaya about motherhood and career, she once told me, "I actually see it differently mom. I do not think that you should wait for the right moment when it is opportune to start having children, because there is no such moment. New career opportunities will always pop up. As I see it, you should first make a decision whether or not you want to have children. And when you decide to have children, then you factor this in when building your career." Both Ligaya and Elena are blossoming in their respective careers, and this goes perfectly well with their being mothers.

In the many discussions about women emancipation, I often get the impression that emancipation is seen as a 'struggle between men and women', that women should be able to prove that they are better than men, that women should surpass the men, that emancipated women no longer need the men or that they can do without the men in their lives. I see this however differently. To me emancipation is to become who you are as an individual, but not disconnected from your social environment and context. So, when you have a partner, your emancipation process should also include your partner's emancipation process. Otherwise, the relationship will not hold.

Emancipation is also something you pass on to your children. My mother gave me the space to become the person that I am, even when that was sometimes difficult and painful for her. I also followed her example and did the same to my daughters.

2019 marked the one hundred years of universal suffrage in the Netherlands, when women also got their right to vote. Though sad to know, after one hundred years of suffrage for women, the political participation of women still lags behind that of men. After the national elections in 2017, only thirty-five percent of the Members of Parliament were women (this was forty-one percent after the 2010 elections). In the local councils, only twenty-eight percent are women. There is therefore still a lot to be done to improve the political participation of women in the Netherlands. The political arena is really still an 'old boys' network', and for women to enter this arena they have to equip themselves to be able to handle 'the rules of the game'. Efforts at stimulating women to participate politically are therefore mostly directed at giving them trainings on debating, learning to present their political standpoints well, and learning the 'rules of the political arena'. While I think that all these are important, that women should learn how to thrive in the male-dominated political arena, I however believe that it is also important to find out how women conduct politics and make this more visible. I believe that an important part of getting more women to participate in politics is to change the current way of conducting politics, away from the patriarchal manner wherein power plays a central role. And I do believe that there is a lot to gain from the society as a whole if women's way of conducting politics will gain more ground in the political arena.

Chapter 24
Musing over a Cup of Caramel Macchiato

"Self-knowledge is achieved not by focusing on yourself but precisely by paying attention to others and to your environment."

I needed to kill time while waiting for my train, and Starbucks was a good place to go to, where I love their caramel macchiato (clarification: this is not a Starbucks advertisement). I did not have a book with me, and I am not good at sitting still. For me, simply enjoying a cup of caramel macchiato was 'sitting still'. So, I started thinking things… philosophizing. My high school friend showed how well she knew me when she described me in our high school yearbook as, "She loves to ponder on the mystic entanglements of life."

What did I philosophize about this time? The paradox of self-knowledge, self-awareness. In the Netherlands (and I think, in many Western cultures) we have learned to direct ourselves inwardly: Who am I? What moves me? What are my drives? What do I want? What do I want to achieve? Where do I want to go? In order to develop, we regard self-knowledge and awareness to be of utmost importance. This makes us assertive, so that we do not simply disappear into the crowd.

But is this how it really is? I have asked myself these questions for so long and so often, that I have come to the point that these questions do not reveal anything new anymore about myself. When I was still living in the Philippines (I was, naturally, then quite young. I was twenty-five years old when I left for the Netherlands), I never asked myself these questions. Does this mean that I then had little or no self-knowledge, and self-awareness? I do not think so, at least it did not feel like it was. I was always sure of what I was doing. Although I never asked myself the question if what I did was what I really wanted to do. I simply did things because they were meant to be so, based on my involvement with others, or in the service of something outside of myself.

Acting out of involvement with others or in the service of something (e.g., an ideal) outside oneself is not disappearing into the crowd; but rather making yourself count, taking your place in what you are a part of. Self-development does not stand by itself, but only has meaning (in my opinion) if it is done to serve something. Thus, you achieve self-knowledge precisely by doing something for others or for your environment. The more you turn inwards, the more you lose yourself. In conclusion, stop thinking what more you can achieve for yourself, or how you can further develop yourself. Rather, think of what more you can do for others, and act accordingly. Only then you will get to know more about yourself and continue to develop your potentials. And at this point in my philosophizing, I remembered a slogan from my student times in the Philippines, which we often used during our protest actions against the dictator Marcos, "Ask not what your country can do for you, but what you can do for your country." (US President John F Kennedy).

It was time to take my train, and while walking towards my train, I thought to myself "I guess I need to de-Westernize myself a little bit."

Chapter 25
Creating and Re-creating Identities

'An important part of me will always be Filipino.'

It was August 13, 1983, when I first set foot in the Netherlands. According to the weather reports I read before my departure from the Philippines, there was supposed to be a heat wave going on in Europe. But when I got out of Schiphol Airport early in the morning of August 13, 1983, I shivered from the cold. It was a chill that I had never felt before, the cold penetrated to the depths of my bones. In the years that followed, like the cold which penetrated to the depths of my bones, the culture and the circumstances of my life in this country continued to have an impact on my very person, such that I would be constantly creating and re-creating my identities.

Carlo and I were deployed to the Netherlands by the Philippine liberation movement to do international work in Europe. I came to the Netherlands with one main purpose, that of gathering support for the struggle of the Filipino people in the Philippines for a just and democratic society, both from Filipino migrants and Europeans. So, my life revolved on the Philippines. I was simply a Filipino political activist doing work for the Philippines overseas.

Migrant
In the course of gathering support for the struggle in the Philippines I interacted with a lot of Filipino migrants, in the

Netherlands and in the rest of Europe. My consciousness as a migrant gradually developed. I realized that migrants also had their own problems in their respective host countries, such as discrimination, racism, having a disadvantaged position because of being a migrant, language difficulties, cultural differences, etc. I saw these problems then as individual problems, which needed to be solved on an individual level.

In 1990 I researched the Single European Act (SEA), also known as 'Europe 1992', which aimed to establish a single European market by the end of 1992. At around the same period that the SEA was adopted (in 1986), the Schengen Accord was also passed (in 1985), and a few years later (in 1990) the Schengen Supplementary Agreement. These treaties stirred various migrant communities throughout Europe, as they meant stricter policies on migrants. I realized then that Europe as an institution was not actually friendly to migrants; that measures were constantly being made to keep at bay the flow of migrants to Europe. Realizing this, I felt that migrants were actually not welcome in Europe, and this included me being a migrant. So, my consciousness as a migrant grew. I realized that the problems migrants were facing could not only be solved on an individual level, but also on a systemic and societal level.

Affinity with Poor and Disadvantaged
In October 1993 I got my first regular job in a Dutch institution that did social work in the city I lived in, Tilburg. I worked as a program coordinator of a parenting program for parents with young children living in the disadvantaged neighbourhoods in the city. This work gradually exposed me to the poor and disadvantaged section of Dutch society. I realized then that it was not only the migrants who lived in disadvantaged positions, but

that there were also sections of the white Dutch population who lived in poverty and had the accompanying social problems. I began to develop an affinity for this section of the Dutch populace. I guess my ideal of fighting for the plight of the poor and the disadvantaged weighed more than just that of my being a migrant. I felt affinity for the poor and disadvantaged, be they migrant or Dutch.

The parenting program I was coordinating was originally developed for migrant families, so that the children of migrant families may overcome their disadvantaged position in Dutch society. But I proposed to the head of our team that we also include white Dutch families in the program. This would contribute to a positive interaction between the migrants and the white Dutch populace in the neighbourhood. In the course of my work, I realized that white Dutch families also had their problems. In fact, I had the impression that their problems were far more complex. With the migrant families, the problems were quite straightforward, mostly related to their being migrants (i.e., language difficulties, inadequate understanding of the Dutch culture and system, etc.). But with the white Dutch families who had lived for years on social welfare allowances, the problems I saw were far more complex—drug addiction of one or both parents, excessive gambling, having unmanageable debts, social isolation, distressed single parents, children caught in the tug-of-war between divorcing parents and even child abuse. Having seen this I made an appeal in one of our team meetings, that we should also do something to help the white Dutch families. After that particular meeting though I felt a bit disturbed. I found it a bit strange why a migrant (two of the program coordinators were white Dutch, while two were migrants) had to be the one to make an appeal for the poor white Dutch families. It felt like I was turning my back on my migrant identity.

Later I would discover that it was not easy for most Dutch to accept that other Dutch also face complex social problems. In a conversation I had with a colleague, a Dutch social worker, she told me that she could not even convince her own mother, and more so the policy makers of our local government, that such complex problems do happen in Dutch homes. But if you say that these problems occur in migrant families, then nobody questions you.

Having realized this, I understood why some poor white Dutch would feel that they are being discriminated against, when they see that most social programs are directed at helping the migrants and not them. This gave me a different perspective in looking at the problem of discrimination and racism: it is not only a race question but also more of a class question. I remember what one school principal (of one of the elementary schools participating in our parenting program) once told me, "You and I have more things in common, we can discuss things more on the same level, than I can with other white Dutch people"—i.e., the white Dutch people who have a low educational level. The class differences in the Netherlands are based on educational level, while the class differences in the Philippines are based on wealth.

As a migrant I can identify myself with the disadvantaged section of the Dutch society, but as somebody with a high educational level (I finished a Master's degree in Tilburg University) I do not actually belong to the disadvantaged section of this society. Quite a strange feeling actually.

Into Dutch Politics

In 2000 I became interested in Dutch politics. I thought that the best way to know more about the ins-and-outs of Dutch politics was to become a member of a Dutch political party. With my past involvement in the left political spectrum in the Philippines, I naturally looked into the left spectrum of the political parties in the Netherlands. These were the Socialist Party (SP), the Green-Left Party (*GroenLinks*, GL) and the Dutch Labour Party (*Partij van de Arbeid*, PvdA). I chose to be a member of the PvdA. My reasons for this were quite simple—SP was too focused on things not going right, I found GL too intellectual or especially represented the highly educated of Dutch society, and I saw that PvdA represented quite a good cross-section of Dutch society including the migrants.

When I signed up for membership of the *PvdA* I did not intend to be an active member. I just wanted to receive their newsletter and other information and materials. But sometime in 2001 I had a meeting with the party leader of the *PvdA* in Tilburg, Jan Hamming, who was also an alderman in Tilburg. I thought that Jan Hamming wanted to talk about the parenting program I was coordinating in several neighbourhoods in Tilburg. Earlier that year I had talked to him about the program, to get his support for it. But when I talked to him, he told me that the reason why he wanted to speak to me was to encourage me to run for the coming local elections for city councillors in 2002, under the party list of the *PvdA*. He saw that I was very involved in the communities where I was working and told me that the party needed socially engaged people like me. To make the story short, I ended up quite high in the list for a newcomer to the party. I was not immediately elected after the local elections in March 2002, but I was the next-in-line. After a year, one of the city councillors of our party resigned. I was then sworn into office as a city councillor in June 2003. I again ran for the local elections in March 2006 and was elected for a second term until March 2010.

As a city councillor I formed a deeper understanding of

poverty in the Netherlands and learned more about the many aspects of Tilburg—its social landscape, its economic ambitions, how it grappled with its urban planning and traffic flow, its many cultural talents, and the involvement of its people in shaping the future of their city, to name a few. Not less important, I also learned a lot about the workings of democracy, and responsible and transparent governance. It was in this period that Tilburg became my city, and with this the Netherlands became my second home.

Philippine Development Work

As I became more and more a Tilburger, my heart continued to beat for the Philippines. This to me is the essence of my being a Filipino. While I may be very well integrated into Dutch society, my Filipino roots will always find its way to manifest itself. And you may call it the workings of the universe, but in April 2011 a good friend of ours, Nonoy Ty, also a Filipino migrant in the Netherlands, asked us if Carlo and I would help him with the work he started in his hometown of Palimbang, Sultan Kudarat in southern Mindanao in the Philippines. Armed with his vision of 'from brain drain to brain gain' (that is, Filipino migrants bringing back knowledge, expertise and insights for Philippine development) he started several initiatives in his hometown several years earlier to help uplift the lives of the people. I saw this as an opportunity to again involve myself in the Philippines, now focusing on development work. In January 2012 Carlo and I visited Palimbang, Sultan Kudarat, and its people immediately captured my heart.

In the years that followed we further developed, together with Nonoy and *Pasali*, our vision for Philippine development, achieving lasting peace and helping poor communities get out of poverty. A vision which goes further than NGO (nongovernmental organization) work. This has resulted in our concept of social business and inclusive business, models of development which we are trying to develop and implement to this very day.

As I look back from 1983 when I first arrived in the Netherlands up to this day, I guess I have completed the circle of creating and re-creating my identities. I started as a Filipino political activist doing work for the Philippines in Europe. Then I became a Filipino migrant, and later became part of the bigger migrant community in Europe. Then I developed an affinity for the poor and disadvantaged white section of Dutch society and learned to understand and deal with the political and social landscape, resulting in becoming city councillor. Finally, I touched base again with my roots, the Philippines. It was quite a journey, but it made me realize that no matter how integrated I may be in Dutch society, contributing and participating fully in this society, does not make me less of a Filipino. An important part of me will always be Filipino.

Chapter 26
Being a Lola

The Lola-grandchild kind of love is a 'love in progress'.

While I scribbled my notes for this article, my then two-year-old grandson Manuel was lying on the sofa in the living room. He finally fell asleep for his afternoon nap after furiously refusing to sleep on his bed. Yes, that's the type of Lola I am, I give in easily to my grandchildren. If he was not in the mood to sleep in his room, then so be it. I let him sleep on the sofa instead. Though honestly, I had to hold him in my arms for about twenty minutes to put him to sleep. I saw that he was already tired and needed to sleep.

Before I became a Lola, I used to tell Ligaya and Elena that I will not be a Lola who will be babysitting their children. But when Ligaya told me and Carlo sometime in mid-2012 that she was pregnant, the first thing I said was that she should allot a day for me to babysit my grandchild.

On March 22, 2013, Ligaya gave birth to my first grandchild, a granddaughter, Tala. And so, I became a Lola.

Having a grandchild is quite different from having a child. When Ligaya and Elena were born, it was immediately 'love at first sight'. The surge of love I felt was very evident. With a grandchild it was more 'love in progress.' In the first few weeks of being a Lola I was especially overwhelmed with the fact that my own daughter had become a mother herself. It felt like a gift, it was a blessing. Soon enough I took up a day every other week to babysit Tala. In the first few months I actually did it more for Ligaya, to support her in her new role as a mother. Slowly but surely, as I held Tala more in my arms, dancing and singing to put her to sleep (this Filipino style of putting a baby to sleep is not done by the Dutch), I started to develop a deep love and affection for her. When Ligaya was again pregnant with her second child, and later Elena with her first child, I actually already had this feeling of affection for my grandchildren-to-be even when they were still in their mothers' womb. It was as though Tala paved the way for this 'Lola-grandchild' kind of love to develop.

On January 2, 2017, I became a Lola again to a baby boy, Manuel—Ligaya's second child. Of course, this grandson also got a taste of her Lola's dancing and singing to put him to sleep.

And on September 30, 2018, my third grandchild, a baby boy, Noan, Elena's first child, was born. Of course, this grandson had his share of his Lola's dancing and singing to put him to sleep. Though in his case I finally learned to just put him in bed to sleep. It is only when he had a running nose and cold when I would hold him in my arms, leaning on my shoulder until he fell asleep.

Seemingly my leftist political background also found its way in the babysitting of my grandchildren as I would often dance and hum to the tune of the 'Internationale' when I try to put them to sleep. And mind you, they do sleep easily with 'Internationale' in the background.

I babysit one day every other week, together with Carlo—Manuel on Thursdays and Noan on Tuesdays. Tala already goes to school, so I only see her in the morning before she leaves for school and in the evening after Ligaya or Arjen have fetched her from the after-school child centre. After dinner Carlo and I would play some board games with her, before she went to bed, and we headed for home. We actually do not really need to babysit as both Ligaya and Elena have good arrangements for babysitting while they and my sons-in-law are at work. Tala used to go to a day-care, and now both Manuel and Noan go to a day-care too. But I wanted to babysit both of them on a regular basis. I wanted to develop a bond with my grandchildren as they grew up.

When we babysit, I usually sleep the night before in Ligaya's or Elena's house, as both of them live about one and a half hours from where I live. This way they could leave on time for their work the following day. I actually enjoy doing this, sleeping over with Ligaya or Elena the night before we babysit. I enjoy especially our talks before going to bed. We would talk about anything, about work, about what we have been doing lately, about our plans, and of course about the children.

Grandparenting in the Netherlands is quite different from grandparenting in the Philippines. Due to the extended family system in the Philippines, the presence of grandparents is more of a given. Grandparents in the Philippines tend to have more say in the upbringing of their grandchildren. In our case, I guess Carlo and I have already adapted to the Dutch way of grandparenting. We actually do not meddle in the upbringing of our grandchildren. We also take their parents' rules into consideration. Like for example, once Tala asked me if I would buy candy for her. So, I asked her if she is allowed by her mama and papa to eat candies. And she told me "Actually not, only when she gets candies as birthday treats from friends." So, I told her that I will not buy candy for her.

Although I am not also really very strict with the rules. Once, Carlo and I brought Tala to a recreation park. Before going home, we passed by the souvenir/gift shop. I told Tala that she may choose one thing to buy. She did choose one thing, but I noticed that there was also another thing she also really liked. I always have a soft heart for my grandchildren. So, I told her "We can also buy that."

To which she answered "But mama will not allow that. I may only have one thing."

To which I told her "It's okay, this is a special occasion. It is our outing." She looked so happy.

On the other hand, Ligaya and Elena have already accepted the fact though that we will always have our own way of grandparenting their children. When Tala wants to assert on doing something which she is not allowed to do, she would reason out that her Lola would allow her to do it. Ligaya would then tell her "You may do that when you are with your Lola, but not with me." They both also know that I tend to carry my grandchildren a lot in my arms, especially when putting them to sleep. They would call this the 'special Lola treatment'. Most babies in the Netherlands are put to sleep by just putting them in bed.

On school vacations Tala would come to our house for two or three nights. We would then go on an outing with her or to a movie. At home I also spend a lot of time *knutselen* (that is, drawing, colouring and making handicrafts out of paper, cartons, etc.) with her. I always look forward to these moments, and Tala too. If I ask her if she would like to spend some days again at her Lola and Lolo's house, she would readily say yes, and her eyes would twinkle.

Carlo and I decided to let our grandchildren call us Lola and Lolo. The equivalent for Lola and Lolo in the Netherlands is Oma and Opa. So, they would call us Lola and Lolo, and when they refer to their grandparents in their father's side of the family, they would call them Oma and Opa.

Tala is aware that Lola is the Filipino word for Oma. Once I fetched Tala from her school. Tala introduced me to her teacher saying, "This is my Oma." On the way home she told me "Lola, I just told my teacher that you are my Oma, because if I will tell her that you are my Lola, she will not understand it." I told her that it was okay as Lola also means Oma.

Aside from the use of Lola and Lolo to address me and Carlo, I actually do not inject too much 'Filipino' in our grandchildren, unlike what I did with Ligaya and Elena when they were children. I find it enough that our grandchildren are conscious of our being Filipinos. I talk to them in Dutch, and I read Dutch books to them. I tell Tala sometimes though about the Philippines, but more in the context of my childhood. I told her, for example, that as a child I loved to play in the rain. She was so fascinated to hear this. I also explained to her how far the Philippines is from the Netherlands, that we need to travel by airplane to go to the Philippines, and that we also need to sleep on the plane as the trip takes many hours. When Tala turned four years old, we gave her a globe, a very good one. I then showed her where the Philippines is. She found this very interesting. We would play make-believe that we were on board an airplane on our way to the Philippines. Then once in the Philippines, we would go to its many beaches, and ride on a small boat going from one island to another. And when it rained that we played in the rain. Once we played make-believe that there was flooding in the Philippines, and that we needed to evacuate ourselves. I then carried Manuel and Tala (in turns) on my back transferring them from one chair to another in the house. Both of them really enjoyed it, screaming from excitement. This kind of play could really be very exhausting, but

I really enjoy watching them get into their roles in our make-believe play.

In August 2019 we took a vacation to the Philippines, all of us—me and Carlo, Ligaya, Elena with their respective husbands Arjen and Hugo, and all three of our grandchildren. It was the first time for our grandchildren to go to the Philippines. Tala was then six years old, Manuel two and a half and Noan ten months. Manuel and Noan were still too young to really remember this experience when they grow up, but for Tala she was conscious that she was in the Philippines, that it is a different country than the Netherlands, where people spoke a different language, where the landscape, weather, food and everything else was different. Before our trip I was a bit anxious whether Tala would like being in the Philippines. Deep inside me I wanted her to like the Philippines, as this represented a part of me, a part of her Lola. I was then so happy to see her really enjoying herself during our stay in the Philippines. When I asked her what she liked most in the Philippines, she enthusiastically replied "Everything!", then added "Except for the fact that I do not understand the language." And I found it so amusing when she asked me "When are we coming back here?"

To which I replied, "We are still here, and you are already asking when we are coming back?" This was one of my cherished moments as a Lola.

Being a Lola is actually quite energizing. I enjoy playing with my grandchildren, running around, even crawling on the floor, playing make-believe, playing board games, working on a drawing or colouring, etc. Being a Lola also helps me to be updated with the latest technological gadgets. It was Tala who taught me the many other functions of my smartphone other than just texting and calling. I also love our little conversations, and I am again reminded how things could just be so simple, and how we adults tend to complicate things.

Another special thing about being a Lola is seeing your daughters' become mothers. And what I see really makes me happy and proud, because I see two very good and conscientious mothers. So maybe, just maybe, I did well too as a mother.

Part 4
Roots

Growing up with my family in P. del Rosario Street in Cebu City has greatly influenced my future life. My mother showed me that a working mother was natural; my father gave me ideals of fighting for the truth and to seek God. The community was a microcosm of Philippine society—I learned about class society, and I learned how to deal with a wide range of people.

My roots are not just history, I regularly go back on values and insights that I have learned from those times. The ease by which I am able to accept people as they are, without bias; comes from my experience of those times.

My experiences later in life have also have profound effects on my life. I have maintained friendships from my days at the University of the Philippines; my experience with the revolutionary movement has also prepared me for further challenges in life.

Jose Rizal said, "He who does not look back at where he came from will not reach his destination." I know I will reach my goals, since I am always aware of my roots.

Chapter 27
P. del Rosario Street

Our neighbourhood was a microcosm of Philippine society.

I was born on the 23rd of December 1957, in our house in 75-D P. del Rosario Street in Cebu City, Philippines. My three other siblings were born in the hospital; I was the only one born at home. My parents told me that shortly before I was born, my mother was already in the hospital. But it seemed that I did not want to be born in the hospital. After many hours of waiting and there were no signs of me wanting to come out, my mother eventually decided to go home. But shortly after that, strong contractions began. Instead of rushing back to the hospital, my father hailed the midwife who lived nearby. And this was how I got to be born at home. So, I guess it was my choice to be born at home.

My father buried the placenta outside the house where rain water would fall from the roof gutters. My father would tell me often that I am continuously fed and nurtured with rain water.

The street where our house was located was actually a small side road of P. del Rosario Street. It was a dead-end road, so we had to walk to the entrance of our road along the main P. del Rosario Street in order to get transportation. Our road served as our playground. Cars that were parked on our road ran the risk of getting scratched by playing children.

Our neighbourhood was a middle-class neighbourhood. The

children went to good private schools and most of the parents had relatively well-paid jobs. At the end of our road though, there is a small alley leading to another neighbourhood. We called this other neighbourhood *luyo* (meaning back, as it was at the back part of our neighbourhood). So, we called the people living there *taga luyo*, meaning people living at the back. *Luyo* was a relatively poor neighbourhood. Many people living there did not have regular jobs, or did manual jobs for some households like cleaning, washing clothes, simple carpentry work, etc. The children in that neighbourhood went to public schools or cheap private schools where the quality of education was not really good. The children from both neighbourhoods did not play with each other. The children of our neighbourhood considered the children of the *luyo* neighbourhood not good enough for them, and the children of the *luyo* neighbourhood considered the children in our neighbourhood as snobs. So, at a young age I actually already experienced the class differences within Philippine society. In as much as I hate to admit it, I was then part of the middle-class snobs who looked down on the poor.

As we grew to become teenagers, we gradually interacted more with our peers coming from the *luyo* neighbourhood. Many teenagers from the *luyo* neighbourhood would hang around near the small alley connecting both our neighbourhoods. My brother used to also hang out there. But my mother prohibited me and my sisters from hanging out in the alley; so, we invited our friends to hang out in our house, or just in front of our door. On reflection I guess that was a good move of my mother. She could then supervise us constantly.

As a teenager I witnessed various social problems that came with poverty. Some of the young girls from the *luyo* neighbourhood would tell us that they sometimes prostituted themselves to get some extra cash. I also learned that some of the young boys were experimenting with 'drugs'. These were not real drugs such as heroin or cocaine (as they could not afford them), but drug substitutes like cough syrup and glue. I was also then exposed to pornography, as our teenager friends from the *luyo* neighbourhood would bring along with them some pornographic pictures. One time my mother saw that we were giggling outside our house. She then asked us what we were giggling about, so we were sort of forced to show her the pornographic pictures. My mother looked at them, frowned a bit, then returned them to us unimpressed, and continued with what she was doing, not giving us any scolding at all. Since then, I never found pornographic material something to get excited about. So not scolding us just did the trick.

While my mother knew that some of the girls that I and my sister hung out with had prostituted themselves every now and then; she never forbade us from hanging out with them. There is a saying that goes "you are who your friends are". I guess this is not true. While we continued to hang around with girls from the *luyo* neighbourhood who sometimes prostituted themselves, my sister and I did not follow suit. We continued to hold on to our values; but at the same time, we were not judgemental of the other girls who had different values. I guess this was what my mother wanted us to learn. (See Chapter 28.)

As a young girl I also learned to gamble. Some men in our neighbourhood, especially of the *luyo* neighbourhood, had fighting cocks. And so did my father. So, they would regularly hold cockfighting, just in the street. This was actually illegal, as cock fights should be held in official cockfighting arenas with permits. This illegal cockfighting is called *tigbakay*. Of course, those cockfights were not without bets. Since my father had fighting cocks too, I also got interested in them. I even had a favorite fighting cock. So, whenever my favorite cock would fight, I would also put a bet on it. Yes, my father allowed me to engage in betting.

I also learned to play *mahjong* with bets. We had a mahjong set, so people from our neighbourhood would go to our house to play *mahjong*. When I came home from school some young boys from the *luyo* neighbourhood would already be waiting for me, to play *mahjong* with me. So, instead of doing my homework, I first spent my time after school playing *mahjong*. I was actually the only girl who played *mahjong*; all of my playmates were boys.

Another form of gambling which was rampant in our neighbourhood was the selling of illegal Jai-alai tickets, called *masiao*. Jai-alai is a kind of game, and people bet on the players—who would come in first, second or third place. This is then a combination of three numbers. There are ten players each time, so you could just imagine how many ticket combinations you can make out of ten numbers. The regular and legal Jai-alai tickets were quite expensive. So, poor communities made their own version of these tickets which was called *masiao*. The *masiao* tickets were then available for ten cents, twenty-five cents, fifty cents and one peso. As a young girl I saw that it was quite lucrative to engage in selling *masiao* tickets. So, I decided to also open my own *masiao* business. And my parents not only allowed me but even supported me in this! Sometimes there were police raids where they confiscated the illegal *masiao* tickets. But in this neighbourhood news about an ongoing police raid ran like wildfire. My *masiao* tickets were never caught in any of those police raids.

As a young girl, I actually made a lot of money from my

gambling activities.

But when I was about fourteen years old, puberty struck me. I decided then that it was unbecoming for a girl to be engaged in gambling activities; so, I stopped all my gambling activities. Yes, just like that! If I look back at it, I am still amazed how easy it was for me to stop something I no longer believed in. Even if it generated money for me.

In a way, our neighbourhood was a microcosm of Philippine society, manifesting the inequalities of its people and its various social problems. I guess because of this it was easy for me to understand what the political movement was talking about.

While I still recall our old neighbourhood with fondness; as a young child I somehow knew that I would eventually leave that neighbourhood, never to return again. Not because I wanted to leave it, but because that is just how things are. We come and go, we change, we grow.

Chapter 28
My Mother

'She was always there, with her unconditional love and support.'

I think many of us consider our mother to be the most important person to have made an impact on our lives. So, I am not unique in this. But our mothers are special to each one of us in different unique ways.

My friends in our neighbourhood would probably remember my mother as somebody they would fear. When she looked for us, she would just shout out our names standing in the street in front of our house. Our friends would then tell us to run home as fast as we could, thinking that we might get a good spanking from my mother if we did not do so. My mother was also a person who cursed a lot, I think she was even the person who cursed the most in our neighbourhood. So, when you get into a fight with her, like our telephone party line (note: in those days telephone lines were shared by two subscribers) who would hang up their phone so we could no longer use it, be warned that my mother would not hesitate to go to your doorstep and curse you from the top of her voice. Yes, my mother did not care what other people thought about her. She said what was on her mind. She was not careful to choose her words, she blurted it out just like how she felt it at that moment, raw and unprocessed. One time in her anger (or maybe more frustration) towards us her children (well children can sometimes be so hard-headed), she told us that if only she knew that we would be that hard-headed, that she would just have chopped us to little pieces then when we were still babies. Of course, we did not take that seriously. And neither did my mother, as she was half-angry and half-laughing while saying this. Yes, that was how my mother was.

    I always had this feeling that my mother seemed to be ahead of her time. She would always surprise me with how she looked at things. When I was in high school, I had a close friend who got pregnant from her boyfriend. Everybody in the neighbourhood was of the opinion that my friend should marry her boyfriend. In the Philippines, at least in those times, we had these double standards. Girls should maintain their virginity and reserve it for their future husband, while boys may have sexual experiences before they get married. In fact, many of my friends wanted to marry an 'experienced' guy, meaning that they are not the 'first sexual experience' of their husband. An 'experienced' guy they said would know how to treat them 'gently' in bed. So, if a girl gets pregnant, she should marry the guy who made her pregnant, because she is no longer 'marrying material' for other guys. Going back to my friend who got pregnant, her mother decided not to let her marry. Everybody in our neighbourhood was so perplexed with this decision. When I told my mother about this, she told me that she actually agreed with the mother of my friend. I asked her "how is that?" And she told me that you cannot right a wrong with another wrong. "Your friend and her boyfriend are just kids. When they get married, for sure they will have more children. You cannot saddle them with raising a family. That is a big responsibility." My friend delivered and raised her baby with the full support of her mother. When her baby was baptized, I was one of the *ninangs* (godmothers). Unfortunately, I was already studying in Manila then and could not be physically present during the baptism.

Years later, we lost contact with each other. I hope that I will see her again someday. I know that she is doing just fine.

I also remember some of my mother's friends who would visit her at home every now and then. I remember one lesbian friend who would come with her partner. I also remember one woman friend who would always gossip and judged others for their 'wrong doings'. She would then gossip about another friend of my mother who also came regularly to our home. This other friend, would then tell about her many American suitors and her dream to finally migrate to the United States. These three friends who came regularly to our house had very different clashing personalities and characteristics. But somehow my mother maintained her friendship with all of them, accepting them for who they were, and yet without having to gossip along with them. Looking back, I think it was my mother who taught me not to be judgmental of people and to take people as they are.

My mother also had a strong sense of justice. One time when I came home from Manila for the Christmas holidays, I saw that my father's other child with another woman was with us. Yes, my father was a womanizer, I have half-siblings from my father's side, and my father did not make a secret out of this. He thinks that all his children should know each other. Anyway, this half-sister was just a year younger than my youngest sister. So, both of them got along with each other quite well. As it was Christmas, I had gifts with me for each and every one in the family. But since I did not know that my half-sister was around, I did not have a gift for her. So, my father instead gave my gift to him to my half-sister, which was a piece of cloth for a pair of pants. My father then wanted to go to the tailor shop with my half-sister and asked my youngest sister to come along. What we did not know was that my half-sister and youngest sister had a quarrel at that time. It was nothing serious, just a petty quarrel between friends and sisters. So, my youngest sister declined to go with my half-sister to the tailor shop. My father got very angry and interpreted it as a rejection of our half-sister. In anger he then said that he better let our half-sister go home as she was not accepted by us. At that point, my mother stepped in. "Nobody is leaving this house! What they have had is just a petty quarrel between friends and sisters. Do not give any other malicious meaning to it. Let them settle it themselves." And so, my half-sister stayed on with us for the Christmas holidays. The next day my half-sister and youngest sister were already playing with each other as if nothing happened the previous day.

Every year my mother kept a big Buddha piggy bank and every Christmas she would then break it open and divide the money among all her children. Since that Christmas, my half-sister was with us, she also got an equal share of the money from the Buddha piggy bank. When my mother and I were alone I asked her why she was so kind to our half-sister and accepted her into our family. Many women I know would not do this. She then told me that my half-sister had nothing to do with the infidelity of my father. "In fact, as a child-out-of-wedlock she already had to endure judgments of other people and has to bear being called a 'bastard child'. I do not want to add to that. She does not deserve that." Now in recollection, I really admire how my mother was able to put aside her own hurt feelings and do what was right and just.

In 1977 when I was studying in UP Diliman (University of the Philippines, Diliman campus), I became an activist against the then Marcos dictatorship. As that was an underground movement (note: it was illegal to be against the government at that time), I kept it a secret from my family. During discussions within the family, I was quite outspoken about my criticisms of the government. Anyway, due to carelessness on my part (my mother found a document in our house) she realized that I was pretty serious with my activism, and that I was really a member of the underground movement. She shared this information with my father and my father got really very angry, he threatened that I would no longer be allowed to go back to UP Diliman to resume my studies. My mother told me however that I need not worry as I will be going back to UP Diliman. "I cannot agree with what you are doing as it is dangerous and I want you to be safe. But I admire you for standing up for what you believe in. I also know that prohibiting you from continuing with your activism will be of no use, as you will continue with it anyway." In 1980 I decided to work full time for our underground movement.

A year later a member of my youth collective in Manila was assigned to my hometown, Cebu City, to assist in the youth protest movement developing there at that time. As he did not have any family in Cebu City, I told him to get in touch with my mother. My mother received him, and the rest of his new collective, wholeheartedly. They became regular visitors to our house. When they were low of funds they could always go to our house for their meals. When I asked my mother why she did that despite her not really agreeing with what I was doing, she told me, "Because I know that out there, wherever you are, there is also another mother who takes care of your needs. I am just returning back the favour, from mother to mother."

As long as I could remember, my mother had always worked. Having grown up in this environment, combining work with caring for your children was for me a normal thing to do.

So, when I myself became a mother I never even considered the option of being a stay-at-home mom. But in reflection, my mother did factor in her motherhood in her career. She had graduated cum laude in her law school, and she was actually a very good lawyer. Though she did not practice law, she assisted my father with his court cases. My father would often discuss with her his court cases and many times they would even debate on it, which I enjoyed listening to very much. And to my recollection, my mother would always make a point, an angle in the case my father had not looked into. So, I guess, had she practiced law, she would have been a very good lawyer. But for as long as I could remember, my mother only had one kind of job in her whole career, that of a Comelec (Commission on Elections) Registrar. As a young child I could remember hearing several conversations between my parents. My mother seemed to have been offered a higher position several times. But my mother kept on declining these. She would then say that her job as a Comelec Registrar allowed her to combine work and the care for her children. Her work was in a way 'very seasonal', being very busy around election times. But in ordinary times her work was quite relaxed. During school vacations my mother would also take us, her children, to her office. So as a young girl I was already quite exposed to a working environment.

There is one thing which I am very hesitant to write about. But I will write about it anyway. Sad to say, my mother was also a victim of domestic violence. My father was rather hot tempered, and especially when he was drunk, he was verbally and physically aggressive. As a very young child I could remember that my mother would sometimes wake us up in the middle of the night and take us to our neighbour's. These were the times when my father came home drunk. From our neighbour's house I could hear the shouts of my father, things breaking or slammed on the floor and the cries of my mother. We would then beg our neighbour to help my mother, but everybody in our neighbourhood was afraid of my father. Until one time, my brother (he was then I think just five or six years old) came out of our neighbour's house and challenged my father in front of our house to a fist fight. I guess that shook my father tremendously because since then his physical abuse towards my mother stopped. Whenever he got drunk, he would just leave the house.

In my perception as a young girl, my parent's relationship was actually far from ideal. My father was not only aggressive but was also a womanizer. In my young mind I would actually sometimes pity my mother for being so unhappy in her relationship. Since divorce is not possible by law in the Philippines; I would sometimes wonder how women, like my mother, could escape from such a relationship. But somehow my mother did! I remember one day, I was then in high school, my mother called all four of her children to come to the living room. My father was already there. When we had all sat down my mother began with her announcement. "Your father and I are already separated, we will no longer live as husband and wife. I do not have to elaborate on the reasons. But he will continue to be your father, and he will continue to fulfil his obligations to all of you as your father." My father did not say a thing. Wow! Here before me was a woman with so much strength. That memory has stayed with me and reminds me of the strength that every woman has inside her.

So, this is how my mother, in her own unique way, made an impact on my life and shaped me to become the woman and mother that I am now.

My mother died in August 1986 due to cervical cancer. She

would have turned 64 the next month. I think she left this world too soon.

Concluding this article, I would like to say this.

The heart of a mother is accepting. It does not make judgments on her children. The heart of a mother does not know how to forgive, for it does not need to forgive. The heart of a mother cannot be disappointed because it has no expectations.

I know, especially in my youth, I caused my mother many sleepless nights. But she continued to support me anyway, unconditionally. She granted me my own decisions and let me live my own life. Not once did I feel I have to justify to my mother what I was doing. What I did, did not seem to matter to her, she loved me anyway. All I felt was that she was always there, with her unconditional love and support.

Chapter 29
Life Happens

Life is what happens while you make plans.

I guess a major turning point in my life was when I went to the University of the Philippines (UP Diliman) in June 1974. I actually did not intend to go to UP Diliman. My high school friends and I saw this notice in our school's bulletin board regarding student applications for the various campuses of the University of the Philippines throughout the country. The deadline for the application was too close. One of my friends said, "Let's apply!"

To which I replied, "But the deadline is already very soon. We won't be able to comply with all the requirements before the deadline."

And my friend said, "But we can ask permission from our Sister Superior to skip classes today so we could work on our application. A nice excuse to skip classes!" And so, we did.

I was not actually serious in getting to UP Diliman. In fact, when the schoolyear started, I was already attending classes in the Engineering Department of the University of San Carlos (USC) in Cebu City where I lived. But when I received a telegram informing me that I qualified for the UP Government Scholarship, my father insisted that I withdraw my registration with USC and go to UP Diliman.

Being accepted to UP Diliman turned out to be quite a big

deal, and especially so because I was accepted to the College of Engineering which was a quota course. So somehow, this was a recognition of my intelligence and academic performance, as one does not just get accepted to UP Diliman. My father always told me that I was very intelligent. But that was my father. Parents are always proud of their children. But my father was a very proud person, bragging about his achievements, and that included me. So, I took his bragging about me as something which parents do about their children. But why did I need an affirmation of how intelligent I was? Well, for a young girl in the middle of her adolescent years when she was still trying to figure out her identity, a little bit of affirmation of her positive qualities could be a big deal.

    I came to UP Diliman as a petite young girl at the age of 16, coming from Cebu City going to the much bigger city of Metro Manila. Since it was far from home I had to travel overnight by boat (inter-island vessel), I had to live in the university's dormitory for girls, and only go home during school vacations. I then had to learn to live independently, and in a way, experienced complete freedom from my parents. When filling up the registration form of my dormitory, my mother did not put any restrictions regarding my stay. I was therefore allowed to come in late in the evenings and spend my weekends outside of the dormitory with friends. This actually surprised me, knowing that my mother was rather strict. But she told me that she trusted me. My mother trusted me with my freedom! For the first time I realized what trust really means, what it means when trust is given to you. To have freedom felt really great! But right after feeling great about it, it immediately dawned on me that responsibilities came with my freedom too. I realized then that I was now responsible for knowing and setting my own limits. I realized then that I was now responsible for my own safety. I became aware that I will have to deal myself (and me alone) with the consequences of my actions. And that felt pretty scary! So, there I was, a petite, innocent young girl, who set out for the great wide world for the first time.

On reflection, I think my going to UP Diliman was something which just happened. I did not really consciously work towards it. It started as an act of skipping classes in high school. But sometimes, as in this case, those things that happen in your life which you have not planned for are precisely the things which make an impact on you.

During my elementary and high school years, I seemed to only have one purpose in life, and that was to study well in school and get good grades, which I achieved quite well. But when I was in UP Diliman, I gradually realized that learning was not confined to the four walls of the classroom. While the seeds of who I was as a person had already been planted, my going to UP Diliman provided a fertile ground for those seeds to grow and bloom. I had the freedom to determine the course of my life, to try new things, to be bold but also to be afraid, to make mistakes, to discover my boundaries, to act on what I thought was right, to accept the consequences of my actions, etcetera.

My going to UP Diliman which just happened in my life, led to another thing which also just happened, that of being part of the underground liberation movement. I never planned to be part of this movement. This movement just crossed my path. It was my curiosity and later my desire to learn more which brought my life's path to this movement. At the start of the schoolyear in June 1977, the students' protests were revived after having been curtailed in 1972 during the imposition of Martial Law. I got curious about the issues at hand and went to those student rallies and protest actions. Then I wanted to learn more, not only about the issues at hand but of what was really happening with the rest of the country. So, I attended symposia and read the manifestos. And to make the story short, there it was, my life's path crossed with that of the underground liberation movement. And since I do take things seriously, I became quite serious about my involvement with the movement and with my commitment for our vision of Philippine society. So yes, later on I included the movement in my life's plan, when I eventually decided to work full time for it in 1980. Together with this decision to work full time for the movement, Carlo and I decided to get married. So yes, this particular part of my life, working full time for the movement and getting married, did not just happen. They happened as planned.

In 1982 Carlo and I had it all planned. We wanted to start our own family. But we needed the support of both our families to raise our future children. So, we asked for a transfer from Metro Manila to our hometown of Cebu City. This was granted. We then went home in December 1982, ready to be integrated with the movement's unit in Cebu City. But before this could happen, we got word from our unit in Manila to come back immediately after the Christmas holidays as there was a change of plans. Upon arrival in Manila, we heard that we will be deployed, not to our hometown of Cebu City, but to Europe instead. The year before, two cadres from the workers' and peasants' sectors had been deployed to Europe. But somehow, they had difficulties in adjusting to life there. They suffered 'culture shock', whatever this meant. So, they returned to the Philippines. But two cadres were still needed to strengthen the work of the movement in Europe. And so, these were the circumstances of how we went to Europe instead, and in particular to the Netherlands. So, going to the Netherlands happened. We did not plan for it.

Like coming to UP Diliman, and then becoming part of the underground liberation movement, both of which just happened in my life, I did not plan for them, coming to the Netherlands also just happened in my life. I did not plan for it. But these things were major turning points in my life and made a tremendous impact on my life. So, what can I say, life indeed just happens.

Chapter 30
Once upon a Time in Heaven

A story of an old soul and a young soul.

Once upon a time in heaven...
Young soul: "God, when can I finally go to earth and experience life?"

God: "Have patience my child. We need to wait for your mentor as this will be the first time for you to go to earth."

Young soul: "It is taking so long, I cannot wait to be on earth."

God just smiled and went on to attend to his other business. After a while though He noticed that the young soul was no longer around. "Where is the young soul?" He asked around.

"Oh, she went with the last batch who left for earth", replied one of the angels.

"Oh, good grief, she cannot go to earth without a mentor", exclaimed God. And at exactly that moment an old soul returned to heaven after having mentored on earth. He was already scheduled to retire, to spend the rest of his time in heaven. A retirement he truly deserved. God took him by his arm and said "Go quick, follow that young soul. She needs a mentor as this is her first time on earth."

The old soul looked at God and shrugged "Okay, okay, do not panic. I'll catch up with her. I just need to round off some things first."

And so it was, the young soul was born on December 23, 1957, and eight days later on 31 December just before the year was over the old soul was born, just around the corner where the young soul was born.

It was when I watched the Lord of the Rings, the episode in which the hobbits Peppin and Merry mobilized the old trees to help fight the enemy, when I realized that perhaps Carlo is an old soul who was sent by God to watch over me here on earth. The old trees were very slow in coming into action, taking all the time to confer with each other to come up with a decision. But when they did, they were unstoppable and really went for it. Carlo is somehow similar to the old trees. He really takes time to churn and process his course of action, very relaxed, no hurry at all. But when he has done that, he also really goes for it without any doubt, keeping to it no matter how long it takes to reach it. On the other hand, I am like a young soul, very restless, always looking for something to experience, who keeps searching for the meaning of life, seemingly insatiable for what life has to offer. Carlo, like an old soul, seems to have already figured out what life is all about. So, he just goes through life very relaxed, with no regrets, taking life as it is.

Carlo was born into a family with no drama who lived a comfortable life. Seemingly, God made sure that he be spared as much as possible from life's drama being an old soul who was actually already scheduled to retire. While I was born in a family and grew up in a neighbourhood with a little bit of drama. As a young soul I still need to experience some of life's drama. While Carlo was born just around the corner from where I was born, their family moved shortly after that to one of the 'better' neighbourhoods, in a suburb of the city. So, we grew up in totally different environments, his being relatively comfortable and oblivious to the social problems that go with poverty, and mine with a little bit of life's spice (See Chapters 27 and 28).

So, our lives would have never crossed paths. But since he is the old soul whom God sent to watch over me, our paths had to cross. After high school Carlo went to the University of the Philippines in Diliman, Quezon City (UP Diliman). He had already planned for this, much earlier. And me? I never planned to go to UP Diliman (See Chapter 29). It just happened. So, it's like the forces of the universe worked together so that I would end up in UP Diliman, at a crucial stage of my life when I was starting on my way to adulthood. A period when I had to be close to my mentor, Carlo's old soul, so he could watch over me. And that is what he has been doing since then.

As an old soul and my mentor from heaven, he knows that I, being a young soul and being for the first time on earth, have this insatiable yearning to experience and understand life. So, he let me; he made sure that he was around with every twist and turn I made in life and encouraged me whenever I started to doubt myself.

At the start of my activism in 1977 I joined a big rally in the heart of Manila (See Chapter 4). When we were dispersed forcefully by the anti-riot police with the use of water cannons, I together with several other demonstrators were cornered at the footsteps of a closed building. I got pretty scared and thought that I would go to prison. Fortunately, due to the presence of international media people we were allowed by the police to leave quietly and go home. While walking towards the bus stop, still shaking from fear, suddenly Carlo appeared before me. "Thank God, I found you. Come, I'll walk with you to the bus." Before getting inside the bus Carlo said "Okay, you are safe now. I have to go back to look for the others." So, who would not fall for such a guy like that?

Shortly after that Carlo and I worked together inside the underground revolutionary movement. When I got more responsibilities inside the movement Carlo never had any problems with it. Never had I felt any tinge of competition from him. It was like he knew that I needed those challenges.

When I decided to work full time with my activism in 1980 Carlo was rather instrumental for realizing this. We got married! Not really romantic huh? But in the Philippines (at least at that time) when one gets married one becomes independent from one's parents. So, even if my parents were against my activism, they could no longer stop me from doing so since I was already married.

When both Carlo and I decided to stop with our involvement in the revolutionary movement in 1993 (See Chapter 6), I continued to develop my career within the Dutch society. Carlo was all the time, even to this day, very supportive, taking on more responsibilities at home, so I will have more time for my career and for my many social and political activities among the Filipino migrants and in Dutch society. Never had I felt that I was being slowed down by him. In fact, he marvelled at seeing me grow and develop to become the person that I have become. He marvelled at hearing my stories about my work and other activities when I came home in the evening. As an old soul and my mentor from heaven, he was only happy to see me grow and have a taste of life on earth.

Of course, I have also exasperated him a lot of times. In my enthusiasm to get the most out of life I could really get so excited on an undertaking, my 'personal projects' so to speak. I would also then get Carlo to get excited about them, only to end up with him motivating me to pursue my 'personal project' to the end, as my attention already moved to another 'personal project' or because I have become discouraged to pursue it to the end. Just imagine, an old soul trying to keep up with the energy and fickleness of a young soul.

On a spiritual level, both Carlo and I are not really that religious in the sense that we do not really attend Mass diligently. But as an old soul Carlo seems to have a complete trust in God that things will always turn out right for us. I, as a young soul, am still trying to figure out how to connect to God. When I worry a lot about something Carlo would tell me "Just be calm, things will turn out right as it should be, God will provide." He would then jokingly tell me "Oh child, you of little faith." I would shrug and laugh every time he said this. But if I really look back, while I may have encountered difficulties in life, things always turned out well. I have a lot of things in my life to be very grateful for. So perhaps, Carlo is really an old soul who has already understood God's ways (or at least many of them), while I am still a very young soul still searching for life's meaning on a spiritual level.

I think each of us has an old soul at our side in our journey through life. I am happy to have found mine.

Part 5
Touching Base

In a sense, I have not really fully left the Philippines, even if I have been living in the Netherlands for more than three decades now. In the early years of my stay, I was part of the Philippine revolutionary movement. From the beginning, I have been working with, and for, fellow Filipinos in the Netherlands. This continuous contact with Filipinos and the Philippines was my way of grounding myself while I struggled to find my place in the Netherlands.

Now, I have added another dimension to 'touching base'. I am now involved in various aspects of the work of *Pasali* (in General Santos City, Sultan Kudarat and Sarangani). I am helping them in the work of fighting poverty in one of the poorest regions of the Philippines.

Touching base with fellow Filipinos and the Philippines has helped me in chasing the windmills of my life.

Chapter 31
With Filipinos in the Netherlands

'My activities in the Filipino community were a stable base to reach out to Dutch society.'

One of the research findings in my Master's thesis (See Chapter 8) was that membership in Filipino organizations seems to play a valuable role in the integration process of Overseas Filipinos. This seems to be true in my case. My activities within the Filipino community in the Netherlands somehow provided a stable base for me to 'reach out' to Dutch society, without having to fear that I will lose my Filipino identity in the process.

Silangan

Almost from the beginning of my life here in the Netherlands, I have been involved with the Filipino community. In 1984, I came into contact with some Filipinos in the city of Nijmegen (which is an hour away by train from Tilburg, where I live), mainly Filipinas married to Dutch. They were thinking of organizing themselves, and a Filipino priest, Fr. Oscar Ante who was at that time doing his PhD in Nijmegen, asked me if I could help them. I participated in their initial discussions. I guess I was quite actively participating, since I ended up being elected to be one of the organization's founding officers—as secretary. The organization's name was *Silangan* (which means 'east' in Filipino) because Nijmegen was in the country's east.

Many Dutch husbands also participated actively in the discussions about setting up the organization. One point of discussion was whether the organization to be set up should be just a Filipino organization or a Filipino-Dutch organization. After some discussions, it was finally decided that it be a Filipino-Dutch organization (that is, the Dutch husbands will also be included), but that it would be led by the Filipinas. So, all the officers were Filipinas. The Dutch husbands only had a supporting role.

At that time, I was still active in the liberation movement for the Philippines. But even if one of our objectives in the movement was to gather political support for the Philippine struggle from the overseas Filipinos, I never injected any politics in *Silangan*. I really just wanted to help them set up the organization, and when it was running well, I relinquished my function as secretary.

Between 1983 and 1993, my work with the movement took up most of my time. Right after the Split from the movement in 1993, I became more involved with the Filipino community.

Tinig

I was one of four people who set up a newsletter for the Filipino community, which we named *Tinig ng Pilipino* (Voice of the Filipino). We launched *Tinig* in 1993. There was already an established community newsletter called *Munting Nayon*. But we felt that there was a need for another type of newsletter for the Filipino community in the Netherlands.

Tinig was different. It sought to unite the community. It was not a commercial operation. It came out every two months. At every issue, we would feature one organization. We ended up discovering a lot of organizations, many from the far-off provinces, as well as foundations that were helping the Philippines in various ways. In *Tinig's* five years of existence, we did not run out of organizations to cover.

We had news from the Philippines, and news on community events. We also had a page in *Taglish* (mixed Tagalog and English), which talked about *showbiz tsismis* (showbiz gossip) and other light matters. We did not focus on private parties, but on the activities of organizations or of the Philippine embassy.

I did a lot of the profiling of organizations: interviewing their officers and attending the organizations' activities. This often meant going far to where these organizations were based. Sometimes I would sleep overnight in the house of one of the organization's officers or members. This gave me more insight into the lives and situation of overseas Filipinos in the Netherlands, as we would then be chatting until the wee hours of the night or the following day before I head for home.

Bayanihan

In 2000, I became the chairperson of the Board of the *Bayanihan* Foundation, after having been a member of the Board for a while. Before this, I had already been active for years in *Bayanihan* as a volunteer for its various activities and services. *Bayanihan* is a women's organization that helps other Filipinas in the Netherlands. It organizes seminars and workshops on topics that would help Filipinas e.g., intercultural communication (i.e., communicating with their husbands), the Dutch education system (to help their children), about work and career development, women empowerment, etc.

Bayanihan also does direct interventions to help Filipinas in trouble. This could be a Filipina with a child suddenly left by her partner, or an *au pair* stuck with an abusive host family. We also counselled couples with marital problems. Not only Filipinas had problems with their Dutch husbands, but the Dutch also had problems with their Filipino wives. A common problem they had was that they did not understand the 'silent treatment' from their wives when they quarrelled. All of a sudden, their wife does not talk to them anymore, and they have no way of finding out what they did wrong, or if their wife had psychological problems. They were relieved to learn from us that this was a usual way for many Filipinas to fight.

As chairperson of the board, I helped in the professionalization of *Bayanihan's* capacity as an organization. My experience in working in a Dutch institution was very helpful in this, as I could transfer to *Bayanihan* what I had learned from it, such as formalizing working agreements with *Bayanihan's* paid staff and volunteers. I also gave some trainings to *Bayanihan* volunteers, to help raise the quality of *Bayanihan's* interventions.

I stopped as *Bayanihan* chairperson in 2005. My work as city councillor in Tilburg already demanded a lot of my time. From time to time, until now, *Bayanihan* would still ask me to conduct a training, or perform tasks in their workshops or seminars.

Pasali

In 1998, Carlo and I joined Nonoy Ty in *Pasali*. Nonoy had set up this organization in 1994 as the Philippine Association of Sea-based Workers for Savings Loans and Investments (or in short, *PASALI*). Later we just called it simply *Pasali*. In 1998, we transformed *Pasali* from a savings and investment association into a cooperative with a remittance business, which we called '*Pasali Padala*'. The members of the *Pasali* association invested the money to set up *Pasali Padala*.

Pasali Padala specialized in remittances to the Philippines by Filipino seamen and other Filipinos. *Pasali Padala* had a network of collectors who received money from Overseas Filipinos (mainly seamen) to remit to the Philippines. *Pasali Padala's* collectors would board ships and facilitate the seamen's remittances, saving them the 'trouble' of having to go to the city centre to remit money to the Philippines. And the remittances would arrive mostly within two days, which at that time was exceedingly fast. And for a low remittance fee.

Pasali Padala partnered with the Asia United Bank (AUB) in the Philippines for its remittance business. We offered bank-to-bank transfers, pick-up at an AUB branch, or door-to-door delivery of the money.

Pasali Padala also sold telephone cards for long-distance calls. With these cards, people could call to the Philippines a lot cheaper than by direct dialling.

The '9/11' events of 2001 (the bombing of the World Trade Centre in the US), and the resulting 'war on terrorism' prompted Central Banks throughout the world to tighten their rules on money transfers. The Netherlands Central Bank made the rules for remittance operations stricter—including high reserve requirements, reporting requirements, and requiring the setting up of a physical exchange office. *Pasali Padala* could not comply with the new requirements and decided to stop operations in 2002. In the period in which it operated, *Pasali Padala* had facilitated remittance worth one and a half million euros to the Philippines.

Filipino Mass

Filipinos in Tilburg and surrounding towns have a Filipino mass (it is officiated by a Filipino priest) once a month. Between forty to fifty people would attend this mass. Carlo and I went to this mass since about the year 2000. In 2013, the person who had been organizing it became sick and could not do it anymore. A group of regular church-goers took over the task of organizing it, and I was one of them.

We decided not to set ourselves up as a formal organization (e.g., a 'Filipino Catholic Community'). Instead, we just divided the tasks that needed to be done among ourselves; and if new people wanted to help, we would accept their help. So, there would be someone who prints the missiles, there is a treasurer, etc. My task is to help with the accounting, and to make announcements at the end of the mass. Part of the announcements are the quarterly financial reports. We find it important to practice transparency in the group.

We organize a disco evening every year in order to raise money (the collections during the monthly mass were not enough) to cover the expenses for holding the mass, such as the rent for the church and stipends for the priest.

The Filipino Mass also has a social function, as we would have a simple *salo-salo* after the Mass, the food provided by the church attendees.

Chapter 32
Healing the Wounds of War

"Getting communities to work together to improve their lives is the best way to build peace." Nonoy Ty, 2011

When I went to Palimbang, Sultan Kudarat province for the first time in January 2012, I noticed an old man walking absent-mindedly everyday along its shores. People called him 'Kaka'. I learned that Kaka lost all of his family during the Malisbong massacre of 1974. More than 40 years after this massacre, Kaka's case demonstrates the deep wound that this event left on the people of Palimbang.

On September 24, 1974, soldiers of the Philippine Army's Fifteenth Infantry Battalion descended on barangay Malisbong and herded more than one thousand men into the local mosque. The military had an ongoing operation against guerrillas of the Moro National Liberation Front (MNLF) in the nearby mountains, and civilians had also fled there to avoid the fighting. The military had assured the civilians that they would be safe, so they returned to Malisbong. All of those men in the mosque were subsequently shot dead. The women and children were brought to Philippine navy vessels anchored offshore; many of them were raped and subsequently killed.

The Malisbong massacre was the most notable event in the war-ravaged history of Palimbang. Through the years, battles between *Ilagas* (a paramilitary group of Christian settlers) and the MNLF, and raids by various other paramilitary groups, had devastated the town. People's properties were burned down. The farmers really had it bad—whenever fighting broke out, they had to evacuate, leaving their lands unattended and their crops unharvested. The debts that they incurred grew to the point that many became tenants on what used to be their own lands.

The period of war extended from the 1970s till the year 2000, when the last evacuation took place. When it was over in 2001, the town was exhausted. Many houses and buildings had been burned down and destroyed. Most of the people were deep in debt. Ricelands were laid idle—it is worst in barangay Malisbong, where former rice lands have turned wild—they had been idle for so long.

In April 2011, a good friend of ours, Nonoy Ty, also a Filipino migrant in the Netherlands, asked us if Carlo and I will help him with the work he started in his hometown of Palimbang. Armed with his vision of 'from brain drain to brain gain' (that is, Filipino migrants bringing in knowledge, expertise and insights for Philippine development) he had set up *Pasali* in his hometown of Palimbang and started several initiatives to help uplift the lives of the people. Sultan Kudarat is one of the poorest areas in the Philippines. The work that he had started had already developed to a point that new challenges had to be addressed to bring it to a higher level. After having left the Philippine liberation movement in 1993, I saw this as an opportunity to again involve myself with the Philippines, now focusing on development work.

When Nonoy Ty and other *Pasali* members arrived in Palimbang in 2004, they found a people who had already lost hope in the future. The farmers were buried in debt. Due to sporadic evacuations many farmers were often not able to attend properly to their farms and harvest their produce. This meant the loss of income and investments. This eventually led to debts and more debts every time the harvest failed. Most farmers then stopped tilling their lands, not only because they did not have the resources anymore to till their lands, but also in anticipation of the next outbreak of another war.

The long period of war had bred distrust among the people of Palimbang—the Muslim Moros, Christian settlers and the Manobo tribesmen viewed each other with suspicion.

Pasali was faced with an enormous challenge when it came to Palimbang—that of building hope again in the war-torn town. When *Pasali* built its centre in barangay Kanipaan, Palimbang, it insisted that Moros and Christians would build it together. In the first meeting held to plan it, some participants brought along their guns 'just in case'. The two communities gradually learned to cooperate and trust each other as work progressed.

Pasali introduced modern farming methods and bought simple farm machinery such as hand tractors and threshers. It also fabricated simple farm machinery such as rotary weeders. It introduced organic farming, which later evolved into a more flexible LEISA method (low external input sustainable agriculture). The SRI- (system of rice intensification) and the SCI- methods (system of corn intensification) were introduced. *Pasali* was also able to put up several water installations which ran without electricity, the so-called hydraulic ram pump.

Pasali organized the farmers into the Palimbang Tri-people Organic Farmers Association (PTOFA). 'Tri-people' refers to the three communities: Muslim Moros, Christian settlers, and Manobo tribespeople. PTOFA had members from all three groups; its barangay-level groups had mixed memberships. The Manobos emerged from a state of near starvation to having abundant harvests—selling their corn and vegetables to the lowland communities.

Because there were no schools in the upland communities, *Pasali* organized lowland Moros and Christian families to host Manobo children at their homes during weekdays so that they could attend school.

Pasali conducted trainings among the youth on operating simple metal working machinery (which were donated from the Netherlands). Among the trainees were former child soldiers.

Pasali has accomplished a lot since 2005, but what the war destroyed in many years could not be rebuilt in just a few years, especially with limited resources. Many farmlands remain idle. The farmers, who have become tenants of the farmlands they used to own, are still not able to get out of poverty. While the production of food has increased, food security has still to be guaranteed.

In the course of its work in Palimbang, *Pasali* has learned that peace building entails more than just a dialogue between the warring groups. Bringing the people together for a common goal—in this case, that of achieving food security and getting out of poverty—gives them the opportunity to learn about each other and cooperate with each other. *Pasali* has witnessed how a war-torn community could build hope for the future together. Hope is what they have together, Christians and Muslims alike. And what you have built together, you will also guard together from being torn apart again.

Pasali is determined to continue its work in Palimbang, specifically addressing the main stumbling blocks for lasting peace—poverty, lack of food security and hopelessness. I am grateful and honoured to be part of this endeavour. These goals have also become my own.

Chapter 33
Pasali and Brain Gain

A new paradigm for rural development?

In April 2011 Nonoy Ty, a good friend of ours, asked Carlo and me to help with the work he had started in his hometown of Palimbang, Sultan Kudarat province. In effect, he was asking us to work again with *Pasali*, which had shifted its work to Palimbang from the Netherlands a few years earlier.

When *Pasali Padala* ceased operations in 2002 (See Chapter 31), Carlo and I stopped with our involvement with *Pasali*. Other *Pasali* members continued by investing in various economic projects in the Philippines. In 2004, they won a contest by Cordaid (a Dutch funding agency) with their idea of 'From Brain Drain to Brain Gain'. Nonoy Ty and two other *Pasali* members used the prize money to start *Pasali*'s work in Palimbang in 2005.

Then in 2011, Nonoy asked us to help out in *Pasali*'s work. *Pasali*'s work in Palimbang, and General Santos City had grown immensely, but it needed to 'go to the next level'. Also, the two *Pasali* members who had gone to the Philippines with him from Rotterdam were no longer able to help, because of health problems.

I told Nonoy that I first needed to see the work in Palimbang and General Santos City before I would decide to help out. We arranged to visit for a few days in January 2012. I saw then that *Pasali* had indeed done a lot of work in General Santos City,

Palimbang and five other towns. We learned about *Pasali*'s Children's Program (which helped hundreds of indigenous and Moro children with their problems and helped send them to school); their urban farming project; their Water Installation work; their Land Redemption Program; their setting up of PTOFA (Palimbang Tri-People Organic Farming Association) with more than 200 farmers as members; and more.

What particularly impressed me was *Pasali*'s work with Palimbang's Dulangan Manobo tribe. Duma Bonifacio, the tribe's chieftain, briefed us about the work that was done in his area. So much had been done including improved farming methods, a corn milling machine, the stopping of illegal logging, the planting of rubber trees, etc. But he was exceptionally proud of the 'school' (then it only offered first and second grades) that had recently been set up. His eyes glowed when he talked about the school, and of the better future his people will face if they would be educated. He was himself illiterate, but he knew the value of education.

The people called him 'Kumander'. I asked why. He used to be a feared commander of the Moro National Liberation Front (MNLF). Previously, the people of lowland Palimbang did not dare to go to the Biao highlands where the Manobo lived for fear for their lives. Then, one day, Kumander approached *Pasali* asking them to consider doing a project with his tribe. *Pasali* was initially hesitant; it had just stopped a failed project with another group of Manobos. Eventually, *Pasali* decided to talk with Kumander's Manobo tribe about the possibility of cooperation with them. In their initial meeting, the Manobos were literally hungry because their hunting party had not returned for a long time (logging had thinned the forest and forced them to go further away to hunt).

With *Pasali*'s help, the Manobos had become self-reliant in food by 2012; by 2014 they were selling corn and vegetables to other Palimbang residents, and even up to General Santos City. Duma Bonifacio died of cancer on July 2, 2017. I feel so honoured to have known him, such a visionary and great leader.

Brain Gain

'From Brain Drain to Brain Gain' is *Pasali*'s call. Overseas Filipinos, instead of being a drain because they left the Philippines, can actually help in Philippine development. In addition to their remittances, Overseas Filipinos can contribute their expertise, know-how, insights, network and resources to help tangible development work in the Philippines. *Pasali* is applying 'Brain Gain' in its work in Palimbang, General Santos City and other towns.

Overseas Filipinos have contributed a lot to develop the work of *Pasali* in the Philippines. It was the money from *Pasali* Netherlands (the prize money, plus personal resources) which launched *Pasali* Philippines' work itself. Engineer Felix Pulmano, one of the *Pasali* members who moved from Rotterdam to Palimbang, made simple machines for the work (e.g., a corn milling machine) and helped bring metal-working machines over from the Netherlands. A former migrant worker from Saudi Arabia led *Pasali*'s Hydraulic Ram Pump installation team. Nonoy Ty has been an able leader of the whole work of *Pasali*: tapping support from within the Philippines and outside; inspiring and guiding all the work of *Pasali*.

And there are the 'little' things. *Pasali* is a very 'horizontal' NGO; its director does not have a separate air-conditioned office. When there is an external training or conference, *Pasali* sends the people who will actually apply the knowledge in practice. This seems obvious, but many Philippine NGOs, would send senior staff for all kinds of trainings. When there was a training on a new rice growing technique called the 'System of Rice Intensification' (SRI), *Pasali* sent three farmers and an agricultural engineer.

Pasali works 'bottom-up', meaning it sets out its plans based on the perceived needs of the communities where it operates, and then seeks support for them. Many other NGOs make their plans based on what is currently 'fundable', based on the priorities defined by funding agencies.

We believe that these and other traits of *Pasali* are because it has continuous input from Overseas Filipinos.

Carlo and I, together with Nonoy Ty have teamed up to be the conduit of this flow of 'Brain Gain' for the work of *Pasali* in Palimbang, General Santos City and beyond. In 2012, we realized the importance of putting the work on an enduring basis, so that it could continue even as funding sources from abroad dwindle. We also looked into ways in which Overseas Filipinos could help with the work.

For *Pasali* to continue its development work on a more permanent basis we saw the need to develop ways of generating funds, such that it will be self-reliant and no longer dependent on subsidies from funding agencies. The idea of setting up a social business came to mind. A social business is one which pursues social goals but is run as a business. Its profits would either be reinvested or go to social projects. *Pasali*'s water installation work (setting up of water ramp pumps) actually already generates income. But for it to upgrade its operations it has to be run as a business, and not as an NGO. We saw this as a way to start the social business. Setting up a business in the Philippines, and much more a social business, turned out, however, to be very difficult. We not only had to deal with bureaucratic red tape, but we were also short of funds.

Farm Machinery
Palimbang farmers have been asking *Pasali* to help them acquire farm machinery to help them with their work. A Farm Machinery Pool (FMP) would lower farmers' costs, increase farm yields, and eventually increase the amount of land under cultivation. We discussed this request and drew up a plan to set up an FMP that would be managed as a social business. This way, the machines would be run by skilled operators, the management of the machines would be run with business-like efficiency, and the profits would go to projects that help the whole community.

We needed to raise around P5 million to buy the needed machines.

The FMP was to consist of Tractors (to plough the fields), Planters and Combi-Harvesters. The tractors would work five times faster than the present hand tractors that many farmers (and *Pasali*) still use (and at least ten times faster than a carabao – water buffalo). The Combi-Harvesters would work five times faster than the current Rice Threshers, and they would reduce wastage during harvest from more than twenty percent to less than three percent. They would also cost less for the farmers.

Raising the money needed to acquire the machines has proven to be extra difficult. Funding agencies which we approached told us that buying the farm machinery is beyond their mandate. The biggest problem, though, was the idea of a social business. They were scared that it would end up being a private business.

Many funding agencies also objected to the idea of using

machinery, because they say that it would leave people unemployed. One agency even suggested that we buy *carabaos* instead, and that they could fund this. This objection of the funding agencies (that is, use of machinery causing unemployment) has, however, no basis. In Palimbang, there is a shortage of people to do the harvesting because the rice harvest time coincides with the tuna fishing season; and local people prefer to work in tuna fishing. Farm machines would also help in opening up land which has been idle for decades.

For six years (from 2013 to 2019), we looked towards foreign funding agencies, Philippine NGOs and government agencies, Local Government Units (LGUs), etc. in a bid to raise money for the machinery pool. Then in July 2019, we succeeded. The German funding agency Bread for the World (BfW) finally agreed to fund our farm machinery. They provided *Pasali* with 1 Tractor, 2 Planters and 1 Combi-Harvester: plus, an Excavator and a (small) dump truck. These arrived when the planting season was already ending; so, they were more fully utilized starting December 2019.

The donation was made to the *Pasali* Foundation. *Pasali* then set up its Machinery Pool as an autonomous unit with independent finances. This is to pave the way for it eventually being spun off as an independent social business.

Molenaar

In 2013, Ka Jimmy, Nonoy Ty's brother, approached us with the idea to set up a rice mill in Palimbang. Jimmy used to manage a rice mill in Palimbang, but it failed because his business partners (all of whom were rice traders) insisted on only processing the *palay* that they owned, and any profits had to be immediately distributed among the owners.

We discussed the idea and decided on a set-up where rice traders, Overseas Filipinos and farmers would have equal shares (each group with a third)—in the investment and decision making. The rice traders would contribute their expertise and business sense, and the farmers serve as base of support for the rice mill project. Overseas Filipinos would provide capital, insights, and be the balance between the first two groups. Each group would invest a third of the needed amount, and each group would have two members on the Board of Directors. Initially, the rice traders were wary of the farmers' participation; and the farmers were also initially worried that the traders would dominate.

We held meetings with the farmers, and they were supportive, even excited, by the idea. Together, we drafted a scheme in which farmers would make instalment payments for five years after operations started. Thirty farmers have now invested in *Molenaar*.

Molenaar is what could be called an 'inclusive business'. An inclusive business is one which is run for the benefit of the masses (farmers, in this case). *Molenaar*, however, goes beyond other inclusive businesses in the Philippines, because the farmers have a significant share in the ownership, decision making and profits of the business.

Molenaar buys *palay* (unhusked rice) directly from farmers for a good price. This price is higher than what middlemen pay for it. It also has a scheme of providing pre-financing to farmers, which are repayable at harvest. *Molenaar* sells the milled rice first in Palimbang; thus, helping to lower the cost of the rice for locals. Previously, traders would buy Palimbang farmers' palay (which is of relatively high quality), have it milled elsewhere, and sell it in General Santos City. Then, other traders would buy low quality rice, and sell this in Palimbang.

Molenaar started milling operations in mid-2017. Its pre-financing program started in February 2018.

'*Molenaar*' is the Dutch word for 'miller'.

Molenaar has had to endure certain challenges in its early days. Traditional rice traders have done their best to deprive *Molenaar* of *palay* to mill by offering farmers a higher price for their harvest. The large-scale importation of rice has led to lower retail prices. This has not hurt *Molenaar* which sells most of its milled rice locally, in Palimbang or neighbouring towns. The lack of working capital is the problem that mostly limits *Molenaar* from achieving a higher production. Much of the capital that it has is tied up in production loans, which means that less money is left for the actual buying of *palay*. Fortunately, many farmers were convinced to sell their *palay* to *Molenaar* for payment a week or two later.

New Paradigm?

Molenaar, the Farm Machinery Pool and the *Pasali* Foundation are the three components of our overall plan to lift the rice farmers of Palimbang out of poverty.

The *Pasali* Foundation (as an NGO) provides services that are essential, but could not generate income, such as: organizing farmers (PTOFA at town level, down to clusters of six - ten farmers at the sitio level); gives trainings on agricultural techniques, financial literacy, run demonstration plots, etc. *Pasali* Foundation's program ALS-EST (Alternative Learning Systems—Educational Skills Training), which initially concentrated on literacy and numeracy training for Manobo tribesmen, also now offers training on operating the various farm machinery.

The Farm Machinery Pool and *Molenaar* provide services that could be run commercially, but for which we have made arrangements to ensure that profits go to improving services and extra income for farmers. *Molenaar*, as an inclusive business has investors—farmers, traders and overseas Filipinos—who will eventually earn from their investment. Some staff of *Pasali* Foundation have also invested in *Molenaar*. The Farm Machinery Pool, as a social business, will not use its profits for personal benefit. Both the Farm Machinery Pool and *Molenaar* will donate part of their profits (as part of their 'Corporate Social Responsibility' allocations) to the *Pasali* Foundation to make it less dependent on outside funding. (Currently, up to 30% of *Pasali* Foundation's operational budget comes from the income of its Water Installation program and its machine shop.) In turn, the *Pasali* Foundation can continue with its programs to help farmers, even when Funding Agencies do not want to support them.

All three components have a significant input from farmers. In the *Pasali* Foundation, farmer-technicians serve as agricultural extension workers. The machine operators of the Farm Machinery Pool come from farmer families. And farmers have invested a third of the capital of *Molenaar*. With farmer participation comes farmer ownership of the whole project.

The capital-intensive components use innovative structures in order to be set up and operate optimally. The *Molenaar* rice mill made use of capital from Overseas Filipinos and entrepreneurs, combined this with farmers' investments, and leveraged all this to get enough funds to set up and launch operations. We set up *Molenaar* to be commercially viable—and this meant that it needed a milling machine that could mill a significant portion of Palimbang's *palay* production, and a large enough pool of working capital to buy *palay* directly from the farmers and provide pre-financing to them so they can plant. *Molenaar* is what is called an 'inclusive business', in that it includes the farmers in the ownership and decision-making of the company, and directly benefits from it (including receiving a share of its profit). This breaks with the traditional pattern of private capitalists, often single proprietorships, to own rice mills. It also breaks with the 'alternative' pattern of NGOs owning small rice mills. Most NGOs who acquire those small rice milling machines end up continually needing (foreign) subsidies to operate, since their scale is too small to be profitable, and they are unable to compete with commercial rice mills.

The Farm Machinery Pool is conceived to be a 'social business' in its full form. In the Philippines, farm machinery is either owned by private capitalists or by cooperatives. Private capitalists will try to maximize their profits and end up charging a lot for their services. Cooperatives, on the other hand, end up being controlled by families (or groups of families) who will maximize the benefits of such equipment for themselves. The social business structure we want will make for efficient operations without the benefits and/or profits going to the benefit of a small group of people. The social business would ensure that the machines are properly maintained, and that the pool of machines will gradually expand to serve even more farmers.

Carlo and I have invested (from money he inherited from his parents) in *Molenaar* as Overseas Filipinos. We have invested the maximum that we had agreed on, which is a twelfth of the authorized capital of *Molenaar*. We regularly communicate with both *Molenaar* and *Pasali* which enables us to make suggestions to improve their work.

We think that the combination of NGO-Social Business-

Inclusive Business is going to be a successful model for raising farmers out of poverty. It is one with maximum farmer participation but utilizing the help of local entrepreneurs and overseas Filipinos in the process. This approach is also robust, and transparent by design. It will not be negatively affected by changes in Funding Agency priorities or Philippine government policy.

If this is successful in Palimbang, we will extend it to cover some other towns where *Pasali* is active. Hopefully, it could be the basis for a new paradigm for rural development.

Chapter 34
Together, we can do it...

Millions of Overseas Filipinos will make the Philippines a developed country.

There were only sixty of them. Sixty young men and women were sent abroad by the Japanese government in 1871, to learn from Europe and America in order to help Japan modernize. Japan had then just emerged from two hundred and sixty-five years of self-imposed isolation. They brought home a wealth of knowledge from the West, laying the foundation for the present Japan—an economic giant in the world.

They were only sixty. The Japanese experience shows what can be achieved when a country's citizens go abroad and learn things that can be adapted and applied in their home country. Of the sixty who went, many became government officials who took charge of various parts of the modernization efforts.

We are in our millions. The Philippines has sent many of us to foreign shores, to work and earn money for our families back home. And we have done this—remitting billions of dollars that keep our country's economy afloat, even vibrant. But this is not the only thing that we send home. We send home values, insights, and a view of the world that Filipinos could not get by just watching foreign films and reading textbooks.

A wise consular official once told Filipinos abroad to "Experience your host country." It would be a pity to have spent many years in a foreign land, and not have learned that country's language, seen its cultural heritage, or learned from its practices and values. We would certainly enrich ourselves in all sorts of ways if we fully "experience" our host countries. At the same time, we are contributing to the wealth of knowledge gathered by all Filipinos who had gone out and experienced the world.

We, Overseas Filipinos, bring back pieces of our host countries constantly—when we go home, but also while still abroad, through our letters, e-mails, social networking postings, blogs. Little by little, the lessons from other countries are seeping through Philippine society. With millions of us abroad, the process is unstoppable.

We can speed up this process by being more conscious in learning what we can from the countries where we are. We can be more conscious in sharing with our *kababayan* back home about what we learn. It does not matter what country we find ourselves in—all countries have some things we can learn from. It does not matter what jobs we do abroad—all of us have something to contribute from our experiences.

Together we can do it. Our millions will become a force that will inevitably help make the Philippines into a developed country in a matter of decades. This is entirely realistic. After all, others had done this before. It is now our turn...

Carlo's Think Pieces (blog), 20 October 2009
Entry for the 2009 Pinoy Expats/OFW Blog Awards (PEBA)

Epilogue

Chapter 35
Dealing with Life After Breast Cancer

'Embracing the effects of my breast cancer as part of me means that IT REALLY IS A PART OF ME'

I started this book describing my emotions and what went on inside me on the day that I heard that I had breast cancer, June 6, 2017. The outpouring of my emotions upon hearing the news, though intense, was quite brief. After shedding a few tears, I composed myself, as if gearing for a new big challenge before me. After talking with the doctor about the next steps to take, I received a handbook with some information about breast cancer and treatments. That handbook somehow symbolized the fact that I was officially a breast cancer patient.

When I came home, I went through the information in the handbook and in some official websites about breast cancer. Going through all that information was for me very draining, as it was not just information, but information that concerned me directly. I am aware of all the information going around in social media and internet about causes and alternative treatments of breast cancer. I even received well-intended advice from friends and family regarding special diets to follow and alternative treatments.

In the midst of all these I told myself that I had to be in charge, for after all this was my cancer to fight. So, I made a decision on which route of treatment to follow—the medical and scientific route. Having made this decision, I continued to gather more information, getting them only from official sources. I prepared for each and every consultation with my doctors regarding the next steps to take by reading through the information I had and making notes on which questions I wanted to ask. One of the doctors, my internist/oncologist, even asked me whether I had a medical background, to which I replied, "No, I just want to be in charge."

In the weeks that followed I underwent several treatments—I had a mastectomy on my left breast on June 29, followed by radiation treatment for sixteen consecutive days (except the weekends) in August, and thereafter started on my anti-hormonal therapy which means taking an anti-hormonal pill every day for at least five years. Fortunately, my tumour was not aggressive, so we decided that it was possible to forego chemotherapy. The negative side effects of chemotherapy would have far outweighed its advantages of treating my cancer.

During this period, I really appreciated the universal health care system we have here in the Netherlands. Because practically everything is covered by the health insurance, I could really concentrate on the treatment of my cancer, with no financial worries to think about. The situation in the Philippines is different. The high cost of treatment is a major consideration people have when making a decision on which treatment to undergo or whether or not to undergo treatment at all. Another thing which I also really appreciated was, that doctors here factor in the quality of life in their treatment plans. So, they do not just aim to get rid of the sickness (in this case my cancer), but they also consider how each treatment could affect the patient's quality of life. My doctor and I talked about this quite extensively, in particular on whether chemotherapy was worth it.

On the one hand it will tremendously decrease the chance for a cancer tumour to resurface somewhere else in my body. But on the other hand, the chemotherapy may also result in other sicknesses since it will tremendously decrease my body's resistance. Not to mention about the pain and inconveniences the treatment entails. The doctor had my tumour sent to another laboratory for extra examination, the so-called mammaprint, regarding its properties, etc. And the results of this extra laboratory tests confirmed the doctors' evaluation of my tumour as not being so aggressive.

Another thing I appreciated very much was how my doctors dealt with me during the whole period of my treatment. I felt I was taken seriously, they took time to explain the treatment and answered all my questions, they listened to what I had to say, and discussed all aspects of the sickness and the treatment every step of the way. They also paid attention to the psychological and emotional aspects of having cancer. In the whole process of my treatment, I felt I was really in charge.

While I did not broadcast my cancer on Facebook, I also did not keep it a secret. I informed the rest of my extended family who were close to me and told them that they may share the news to the rest of the family and to people who knew me. I also informed some close friends and colleagues, and also told them that they may share the news to others who know me. The support I got from family, friends and colleagues was overwhelming. Aside from the flowers and cards, prayers were said for me, and candles were lit. These were all very heart-warming and a feeling of gratitude overwhelmed me.

While I seemed to deal with my cancer in a very level-headed way, a lot of thoughts and emotions were going on inside me. I thought about death, about how I had lived my life so far, and the pain this will cause to my loved ones. It was especially the thought of the pain I will cause my two daughters that broke my heart. I wrote more about this in Chapter 1.

In September, two months after my operation, I slowly resumed my work. By November I was fully back into work and had resumed all my other volunteer activities too. I was then still experiencing the effects of my radiation and my anti-hormonal medication, especially the spells of tiredness and some tinge of pain in the affected area. I understood that this will continue for some time, maybe even for the rest of my life. I therefore made a decision to learn to live with it and embrace it as part of me.

I remember a conversation I had with Ligaya, shortly after I heard about my breast cancer. A Filipina friend of mine, whose daughter is also her friend, died the previous year of cancer, which also started as a breast cancer. Ligaya recalled when she heard from her friend about her mother's cancer. That was about twenty years ago. So, I told Ligaya "Well, if I will also have another twenty years before I die, then that will not be too bad. By then I will be about eighty years old. A good age to die."

On second thought, why bargain for less? Before I knew that I had cancer I actually intended to live until I am ninety years old. So, I have restored my intention to live until I will be at least ninety years old. I guess the dust has settled.

In retrospect I had expected my cancer to dominate my life. But it actually did not. Although, if I feel something unusual in my body or if I do not feel well, the first thing that comes to my mind is cancer. That perhaps it had (re)surfaced somewhere else in my body. And that feeling of fear would take over me. But so far, I have always managed to shrug this off immediately. If there is one thing I hate, it is living in fear.

But how am I really doing?

On the surface I indeed resumed my work and all my volunteer activities quite quickly. I went back again to my quite busy life. For a living, I work with the Council for Refugees (*Vluchtelingenwerk*). Outside of it I do several volunteer activities: as member of the Board of the feminist group (*Rooie Vrouwen*) of the Dutch Labour Party (*PvdA*); as member of the Activities Committee of the Society for Intercultural Education, Training and Research in the Netherlands (SIETAR); and as interim coordinator of the Project Committee for Asia of the Melania Foundation, a foundation which gives financial support to small scale income generating activities of women in developing countries.

In the midst of this 'busy-ness' I also picked up the personal and spiritual aspects of my life. On the family level, I resumed babysitting my two grandsons, Manuel every other Thursday, and Noan every other Tuesday.

Being confronted with cancer also prompted me to really start to write 'my book'. I have been wanting to write 'my book', but this did not really go far other than just scribbling some notes. But when you are confronted with cancer, you suddenly feel that your life has a deadline. So, this prompted me to really pick up that pen and finish the scribblings I made and type that piece in the computer.

In the months of my treatment, I spent a lot of my time at home. A restless soul that I am, our old piano caught my attention, and I started to tinker some notes again on the piano. When I was a child I had a few years of piano lessons, so I can read music notes a bit. My daughters also used to play the piano. So, we have this old piano at home, which was hardly played since my daughters moved away from home. While trying to wrestle with the notes on the piano I noticed that it can really consume me in a positive way. It really gets my full attention, to only that what I am doing at the moment—getting the notes right, setting the right fingers on the keys and figuring out the melody that comes out of it. Wrestling with the notes on the piano brings me to the here and now. So, in a way it is actually like a form of meditation.

I also learned that once I get the notes right, I should just trust my fingers that they will find their way on the piano. On reflection, this process of playing the piano is actually a nice metaphor for life—trust and have confidence in what you already know.

So having said this, I decided to continue playing the piano and am now taking piano lessons. Another activity which I picked up again is long-distance walking. My introduction to long distance walking was in 2011 when I prepared for the Walk of the World in July that year. (See Chapter 14). After that event I actually hardly spent time with long-distance walking. But I have always wanted to walk the Pieterpad, a route from the town of Pieterburen in Groningen up north, to down south, the St. Pietersberg in Maastricht. The whole Pieterpad consists of twenty-six stages, each stage consisting between sixteen to twenty kilometres, covering a total of four hundred and ninety-eight kilometres. To encourage me to pursue this wish, my daughters and sons-in-law gave me a guidebook of Pieterpad for my sixtieth birthday. To help me get started, Ligaya walked the first 2 days with me in April/May 2018, and Elena kept me company at the end of the first two stages that I did in August of that same year. She would have walked with me too, but she was already very pregnant at that time. I did the first six stages in April/May, and the succeeding four stages in August, covering a total of one hundred and ninety-three kilometres. And in April

2021 I resumed walking with four stages, bringing my total to three hundred and fifteen kilometres. I still have a long way to go.

In June 2018 I also participated for the first time in the Night of the Refugee, a long-distance walking event of forty kilometres during the night to raise funds for the care of refugees in refugee camps. (See Chapter 15). In September 2021, I again participated in the Night of the Refugee.

Long distance walking is not just making those kilometres. With the Pieterpad I got to see more of the Netherlands, places that I have never been before. With the Night of the Refugee, you do it for a purpose, something bigger than you. I also did a lot of self-reflection during those long walks, like you're having a conversation with your soul. So, in a way, long-distance walking is also a form of meditation.

My next project is to walk the French route of the Camino de Santiago de Compostela in Spain, starting from St. Jean-Pied-de-Port. This is a route of more than seven hundred kilometres.

So, within almost two years from having been diagnosed with having breast cancer, I was up and about and back to my old me. And so, I thought. I thought that life after breast cancer was simply picking up my life again where I have left it before I was diagnosed with cancer.

But then the spells of tiredness which ensued during my radiation treatment never really left my body. While I understood then that this will continue for some time, maybe even for the rest of my life, I took it as something I will just have to embrace as part of me, and it will not get in the way. I realized that embracing it does not mean going on my old merry way. Embracing the effects of my breast cancer as part of me means that IT REALLY IS A PART OF ME, it exists, and I could not just brush it off. I have to deal with it and accept the fact that it does change my life.

It took me some time to accept this; that I will have to let go of some of my activities. So, with pain in my heart, I dropped my activities for SIETAR and for the Melania Foundation in the Spring of 2019. At the end of this year 2021 I will also let go of my activities for the *Rooie Vrouwen*.

My social involvement has always been a part of me. I even consider it to be in the core of my being as a person. So, letting go of these activities is like letting go of an important chunk of myself. I feel that I need to recreate myself again. I guess this is the challenge I will be facing in this phase of my life.

I will continue to chase windmills. My journey continues…

Chapter 36
About God

'Where there is love. God is there.'

"Where there is friendship and peace. Where there is love. God is there." This is my favourite line of a song often sung in Sunday Mass in the Maria Church in our neighbourhood in Tilburg. To me, this embodies the very essence of God's message for us. Very simple, and yet somehow so difficult to live by, judging by the many man-made sufferings taking place all around the world.

I want to end my book by writing my thoughts about God. Upon reflection, *Chasing Windmills* (my efforts at living my life based on principles) started with my search for God (See Chapter 3). It was my search for God which brought me to the Philippine revolutionary movement, when I found God among the poor and the oppressed of society; and realized that serving them and fighting to uplift their lives is a way of serving God. It was also during my involvement in the Philippine revolutionary movement when I realized that God has always been there and still is present in my life. Even if I did not pay much attention to my relationship with God when I was in the heat of my involvement in the movement, but when Carlo and I were faced with a very difficult situation as a result of us getting out of the movement (See Chapter 6), new opportunities started to unfold. I realized then that God had never really left us. And on reflection, as I went on with my life, I realized that God was always there.

God manifests itself in our lives in many unexpected ways. When I think, for example, about the circumstances around the finishing of my thesis and finally getting my Master's diploma in Psychology, it was actually that chance encounter I had with my professor while I was doing groceries which triggered everything and put things into motion. It may be simply a case of serendipity, but to me it felt like the 'forces of the universe' had worked together to help me finally get my diploma. (See Chapter 8)

God is for many people often equated with religion. In my case though, I have already learned to see both separately at an early age. This was especially due to my father's influence who was very critical about the Catholic Church (I was baptized in the Roman Catholic Church) but had a great faith in God. My observations of Philippine society, in which the gap between rich and poor is so big, also contributed to this realization. It was, for example, not unusual to see rich people diligently going to church on Sundays, and even attend novenas on Fridays, but at home they do not treat their household helpers well. Worse, they look down on and mistrust the poor. So, at an early age I already started to wonder how one could be so religious and yet not feel compassion for the poor. Is not God among the poor?

When I came to the Netherlands, I learned about how the Jews were persecuted during World War II and how the Muslims are still being discriminated to this very day. And if we look into our history, we will see that many killings were done and continue to be done in the name of God. I could just imagine how God would be shaking His head in disbelief when such things happen. We could also see to this very day how various religions exclude each other or exclude certain groups of people like the gays and lesbians. So how could one be so religious and yet exclude others? Are we not all children of God?

So, in reflection, I can only conclude that God cannot be equated with religion. I think, the many religions we have in the world are man's efforts in trying to understand God. I believe that God expresses Himself in love. It sounds so simple, but somehow this seems to be so difficult to do, to love each other, to have compassion for the weak, to forgive each other, to let love rule our lives.

It is often said that God works in mysterious ways, and that God is way beyond us, that God is way beyond our capacity to understand Him. I tend to believe that this is true. Love, which to me is the essence of God, seems so difficult to understand and live by. That feeling we think is love, is actually just a minuscule of what love really is, of what God meant love should be.

If we take a closer look at our lives, we will see that God actually took a lot of effort for us to understand Him, for us to understand what love really is. For instance, I do believe that motherhood (not to say that fatherhood is not, but I can only speak for myself as a mother) is one of God's ways to let us understand what love is really all about. I believe that God's love for us is unconditional, just like my love for my children is unconditional. As a mother I could say that there is nothing my daughters will do that would make me love them less. And now being a *Lola* I could also say, deep in my heart, that there is nothing my grandchildren will do that would make me love them less. I think this is the kind of love God has for all of us, but very much bigger. I feel so blessed and thankful that God gave me this opportunity to understand His love for us by being a mother, and now also a *Lola*. And to make the circle complete, it was my mother who showed me and let me feel what unconditional love is all about, such that I may also give it to my own children.

Having experienced unconditional love, the biggest challenge at hand is to extend this kind of love to all of humanity. For where there is friendship and peace, where there is love, God is there.

In conclusion, since we are all children of God, there is nothing we can do that will make God love us less. For His love is unconditional, the same unconditional love mothers have for their children. So, in the final analysis, I really believe that we all will go to heaven eventually, back to God's home, when we have found love in our hearts and in the hearts of others. For God is love.

www.ingramcontent.com/pod-product-compliance
Lightning Source LLC
LaVergne TN
LVHW091535060526
838200LV00036B/624